Higher ENGLISH for CfE

READING FOR UNDERSTANDING, ANALYSIS AND EVALUATION

Ann Bridges and Colin Eckford

SCOTTISH
EXAMINATION
MATERIALS

HODDER
GIBSON
AN HACHETTE UK COMPANY

The Publishers would like to thank the following for permission to reproduce copyright material:

See back of book.

Every effort has been made to trace all copyright holders, but if any have been inadvertently overlooked the Publishers will be pleased to make the necessary arrangements at the first opportunity.

Although every effort has been made to ensure that website addresses are correct at time of going to press, Hodder Gibson cannot be held responsible for the content of any website mentioned in this book. It is sometimes possible to find a relocated web page by typing in the address of the home page for a website in the URL window of your browser.

Orders: please contact Bookpoint Ltd, 130 Park Drive, Abingdon, Oxon OX14 4SE. Telephone: (44) 01235 827720; Fax: (44) 01235 400454. Lines are open 9:00–5:00, Monday to Saturday, with a 24-hour message answering service. Visit our website at www.hoddereducation.co.uk. Hodder Gibson can be contacted direct on: Telephone: 0141 848 1609; Fax: 0141 889 6315; email: hoddergibson@hodder.co.uk

First published in 2015 by

Hodder Gibson, an imprint of Hodder Education,

An Hachette UK Company,

2a Christie Street

Paisley PA1 1NB

Impression number	5	4	3	2	1
Year	2019	2018	2017	2016	2015

Cover photo © contrastwerkstatt – Fotolia

Typeset in Minion Regular 12/14.5 by Integra Software Services Pvt. Ltd., Pondicherry, India

Printed in Spain

A catalogue record for this title is available from the British Library.

ISBN: 978 1 4718 3806 4

CONTENTS

INTRODUCTION

The purpose of this book is to help with the Understanding, Analysis and Evaluation part of the English exam. But this is only the end point of an educational process that should be valuable for its own sake.

The passages and extracts students are expected to be able to read and understand are non-fiction passages designed for an adult readership. The topics vary but the reading usually involves confronting ideas and opinions about issues of the day. If nothing else, reading this material means students will become better informed about society and its concerns.

Another point is that a considerable proportion of an educated adult's reading is likely to be non-fiction – newspapers, work-related documents, books on leisure pursuits and interests, for example – so it seems self-evident that students should be practising the skill of reading these texts in school or college.

In such writing, the level of vocabulary and complexity of sentence structure can act as a barrier to the simple understanding of these texts. This means that presenting such passages for close scrutiny will, in time, develop the students' ability to read for information.

That is not enough, however, in a world where almost no text is neutral. There is a series of devices commonly used that create bias, spin, enthusiasm or entertainment. The ability to spot and analyse these devices allows the reader to be critical, to appreciate at a more subtle level the communications that come her way. Not only will this make the reading experience richer, the reader will also be better equipped to take an active part in debate and in the democratic process.

That takes care of understanding and analysis. The evaluative process is one that follows on from the previous two, in that it becomes second nature to reflect on a piece just read and see where it has left one's views, one's knowledge and, occasionally, one's temper.

This book is designed to help with the detailed study of reading in the way that it is dealt with at Higher level in English, but the overarching idea should be kept in sight. There are many small trees, but the important feature is the wood.

The first part of the book uses short passages, each of which concentrates on developing understanding and the ability to comment on techniques commonly adopted by writers of non-fiction. There is of course overlap among the techniques used in all these passages, just as there is an overlap between understanding and analysis, and between analysis and evaluation. The topics are varied – from female comedians on TV to the NHS, from bilingualism to robot cars. There are a number of exercises associated with each passage, the answers to which can be found at the end of Part One.

The second part of the book builds on the work of Part One by providing full-length passages for practice. The answers to these are given in the separate *Answers and Marking Schemes* book.

The third part of this book consists of exercises in comparison. This part starts with short examples and simple explanations and questions, followed by longer passages to work through with support. The final examples are exam-style passages for practice.

The last part of the book consists of six double passages for practice in reading and answering questions; these are formatted as in the Higher examination. The topics include such things as Homework and the TV show *Breaking Bad*. There are extensive and detailed Marking Guidelines for each passage in the separate *Answers and Marking Schemes* book.

The materials in the first three parts of this book provide alternatives to the unhelpful practice of churning through complete past papers; they can provide a teaching focus or a remedial focus on individual aspects of reading skills.

The fourth part of the book provides ample practice for the run-up to tests or the examination.

But over and above all this, the practice of reading topical passages, and spotting the interesting ways in which the subjects are presented, should lead on to further reading and analysis. Students should be encouraged to find interesting short extracts that can be the subject of a ten-minute discussion or a short written exercise on a particular technique. In this way a number of topics and techniques can be dealt with fairly briefly in a stimulating way (or before everyone gets bored stiff).

The real objective at the end of a Higher English course should be not just an examination pass, but a mature and interested approach to reading in all its forms.

TYPES OF QUESTIONS

The material in this part of the book is divided into five sections, each of which deals with 'classes' of questions in the Reading for Understanding, Analysis and Evaluation paper in the Higher English examination.

The five sections are concerned with:

- Identification
- Explanation
- Analysis
- Evaluation
- Summary

Each section has two sample passages, with advice and typical questions. There are tasks to be performed and then there is a summary of the ground covered, with a reminder of the technical terminology that has been illustrated in the course of the chapter.

Possible answers to the questions are provided at the end of Part One (page 47). The answers are very full – sometimes seeming to verge on the excessive. They are not the answers that will typically have been produced by the average Higher candidate (although there is proof that some candidates do produce answers that are as fully developed as any in these pages). The purpose of the answers is to cover a variety of possibilities that will help the reader see beyond what they themselves have written and be encouraged to think along the lines suggested by the answers.

The answers are actually very important to the usefulness and scope of this part of the book. There is a wealth of detail and advice designed to complement the initial 'teaching' material in the body of the chapter. There are also, in many cases, commentaries on the answers, which provide useful pointers of a general kind.

It cannot be emphasised too much that the answers are as important for teaching and learning as the original exercises are. Their usefulness lies not in letting students 'mark' their own work, but in showing the kinds of appropriate comments that are acceptable. By constantly being exposed to the terminology and formulae of such successful answers, students will pick up good habits to help them organise their thoughts.

Throughout these exercises and answers there is a wide range of complex vocabulary used. This may stretch the average student, but exposure to these words and concepts should extend her critical vocabulary. This may demonstrate the need to expand the active vocabulary available to the student. A wide vocabulary is needed to provide the connotations, synonyms and 'translations' necessary to answer questions effectively. Students often show in their answers that they have the right idea but that they lack the vocabulary to express what they know. The exercises (and answers) in this book may help a little, but the basic work has to be done by more reading of high-level language. If the only non-fiction articles read by students are the passages in this book and a sprinkling of past papers, then their chances of success are limited.

SECTION 1 – IDENTIFICATION

Typical questions of this type start with an instruction to 'Identify the reasons/ideas/points the writer makes about …'

The purpose of these questions is usually to see that you have been able to isolate ideas and to understand them and their place within the passage. This helps to clarify your thoughts and allows you to see where a passage is going.

Quite often these questions are relatively straightforward. You are not expected to make long comments justifying your choice (unless you have specifically been asked to do so). Simple identification is what is required.

Sometimes you can be prompted to find points because there are helpful signposts in the passage: 'The first thing to notice is …', 'secondly', 'finally', and so on. If you have been asked to find three points, the chances are that you can find them in these little segments.

Sentence structure can also be helpful in separating one point from another. A sentence might begin with a statement about climate change, followed by evidence to back up the initial statement. The following is a simple example:

Climate change is fast approaching, faster than has been hitherto thought: the Antarctic glaciers are retreating at an accelerating pace; the warmer waters are undermining the coastal ice shelf, causing great icebergs to detach themselves more frequently; the consequent rise in sea levels (although at present very small) may reach one metre in this millennium.

Here the three points made – the three pieces of evidence – are quite obvious because the punctuation tells you where one point has ended and another has begun:

- Antarctic glaciers are diminishing fast.
- More icebergs are breaking off from the mainland than before.
- Water levels in the ocean are rising progressively.

One important aspect of this kind of task is that you are expected to recast the information in your own words – as has been done in the bullet points above.

You don't have to 'translate' every single word. You have to demonstrate that you have understood the point, but there is no sense in trying to translate 'Antarctic glaciers' into 'Southern Ocean ice rivers' – an Antarctic glacier is just an Antarctic glacier. You demonstrate your understanding by showing that you know what 'retreating at an accelerating pace' means.

If you had written the three points more briefly, as below, there would be something missing in your total understanding of the points:

- Antarctic glaciers are diminishing.
- Icebergs are breaking off from the mainland.
- Water levels in the ocean are rising.

There is no mention of the speed at which this is all happening, and its speed is one of the important points at the beginning of the sentence: 'Climate change is fast approaching, faster than has been hitherto thought'. This second set of bullet points is just too brief to demonstrate complete understanding.

The repetition of a key word in a paragraph can alert you to a second or third fact associated with the initial idea. Here is an example:

New technology has made it much easier for governments to oversee what people and institutions are up to. Government can now spy on us in all sorts of exciting new ways: read our emails, listen to our phone calls, track our text messages, access our bank accounts. But government being government, it often does this inefficiently and cackhandedly, which makes it even more frightening, given its potential for making wrongful accusations.

If you are asked to identify two aspects of what new technology has enabled governments to do, the repeated word 'government' will show you the beginnings of two statements:

- Governments can spy on their citizens using modern communications systems.

- Governments can get it wrong (because they are not very good at it).

There are two points to notice about these answers:

1. The different methods of communication are generalised under 'modern communications systems'. In this easy example you can see that it would not be sensible to quote this whole list and try to translate each one. The skill of generalisation is important, not only in this type of question, but in the whole business of summarising – going from the details to the main point.
2. The two points are recast 'in your own words'.

Further practice

Robot cars – made by Google

States can do plenty of things that business organisations can't. States fight wars; Google doesn't, and not just because the company motto is 'Don't be evil'. Google lacks the organisational capacity and the absolute authority for war. It couldn't fight one even if it wanted to. A state – the USA – put a man on the Moon, another massively costly

5 enterprise that had all sorts of unexpected technological spin-offs. Google might like to do something as ambitious, but it wouldn't dare be so reckless with its cash. (The Apollo programme cost well over $100 billion in today's money; the space shuttle programme cost twice as much, or more than half the current net worth of Google.) States – thanks to their tax-raising powers – are able to pool resources to a degree that not even the

10 biggest businesses can match.

But businesses can do plenty of things that states can't. Google has just come up with a self-driving car that actually works. It has married its mapping technology to its super-smart computers to produce a machine that performs a complex task far more safely than any human being could manage. Google's self-driving cars don't crash (so far). It is

15 hard to imagine a government programme resulting in a self-driving car that didn't crash. Governments tend to screw up complex, open-ended tasks like that. (The mission to put a man on the Moon was complex, but it wasn't open-ended: it had a straightforward, hard-to-miss target in the Moon itself.) Governments don't build good cars. The hopelessly inefficient and unreliable bangers turned out by the communist states of Eastern Europe –

20 their puttering Ladas, their tin-box Trabants – are witness to that.

Most resources work best when they aren't pooled. Competition encourages diversification as well as innovation. There are limits to what markets can do, however. Champions of the free market have an unjustified faith in their ability to solve any problem. Yes, private enterprise has given us the self-driving car, which may one day

25 have the power to change the way we live. (Sit in the back, read a book, sleep, work out, make out, and suddenly your daily commute becomes the best part of your day.) →

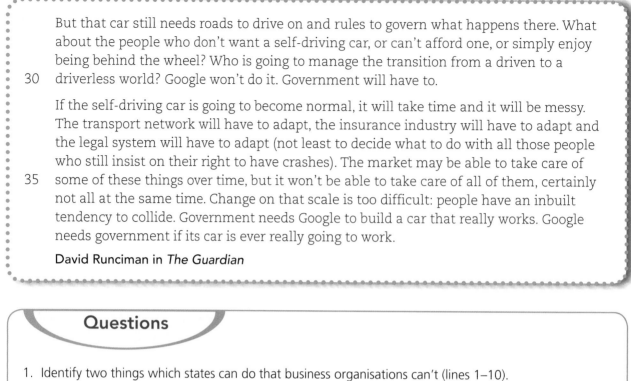

But that car still needs roads to drive on and rules to govern what happens there. What about the people who don't want a self-driving car, or can't afford one, or simply enjoy being behind the wheel? Who is going to manage the transition from a driven to a driverless world? Google won't do it. Government will have to.

30

If the self-driving car is going to become normal, it will take time and it will be messy. The transport network will have to adapt, the insurance industry will have to adapt and the legal system will have to adapt (not least to decide what to do with all those people who still insist on their right to have crashes). The market may be able to take care of some of these things over time, but it won't be able to take care of all of them, certainly not all at the same time. Change on that scale is too difficult: people have an inbuilt tendency to collide. Government needs Google to build a car that really works. Google needs government if its car is ever really going to work.

35

David Runciman in *The Guardian*

Questions

1. Identify two things which states can do that business organisations can't (lines 1–10).
2. Identify two ingredients Google has used to make a driverless car possible (lines 11–20).
3. Identify three problems arising from the invention of the driverless car that government will have to sort out (lines 21–30).
4. Identify three aspects of motoring that will require change (lines 31–38).

In these questions you have been given line references – each of which, in this case, covers a complete paragraph. The actual points required can be found anywhere within these lines, and not all the material in those lines will be needed. Make sure that you read to the end of the reference so that you don't miss anything important. Equally, if you spot the 'answer' at the end of the paragraph, just check that there isn't anything you have missed at the beginning.

As you will see when you look at the answers, some of these questions are really easy and some require a little more thought, but they are generally questions that you can answer quickly and without any further explanation or comment.

Answers

Answers can be found at the end of Part One, on page 47.

Conclusion

This is the kind of question that you should be able to complete fairly quickly and briefly.

Look for signposts, repetition of key terms and clues in sentence structure.

List of terms used

Sentence structure, signposts, generalisation, recasting (in your own words), summarising.

Supplementary passage

How Harry Potter saved one small Highland town's economy

Mallaig's days as a bustling herring port are long gone, but the town is still full of people today. Few would have guessed that its commercial salvation would be owed to a modern fairytale.

The railway reached Mallaig from Fort William and the south in 1901; it was among the last big lines to be built in Britain, late enough to have its viaducts built of concrete by the contractor Robert McAlpine ('Concrete Bob'). It traversed one of Europe's most spectacular and empty landscapes – lochs, mountains, sea inlets, moorland – with hardly
5   anything large enough to be called a village along its 40-mile length. Its construction needed a large – and controversial – government subsidy, and its traffic never grew much beyond the two or three trains a day that carried fish boxes and a few dozen travellers to and from the Hebrides. It made little economic sense. Only 60 years after the line opened, it began to be threatened with closure. Few people would have guessed then that
10 its commercial salvation would eventually be owed to a novel and a film, and first of all, to a hobby.

In 1899, the Railway Club, the world's first society for railway enthusiasts, was founded in London. It was from these elite beginnings that the twentieth century's great cult of trainspotting spread to even the roughest school playground, reinforcing a general
15 fondness for steam locomotives that many people had without knowing quite why, so that a sense of loss ran through Britain (more so than any other country) when, in the 1960s, it became clear that their day was nearly done.

→

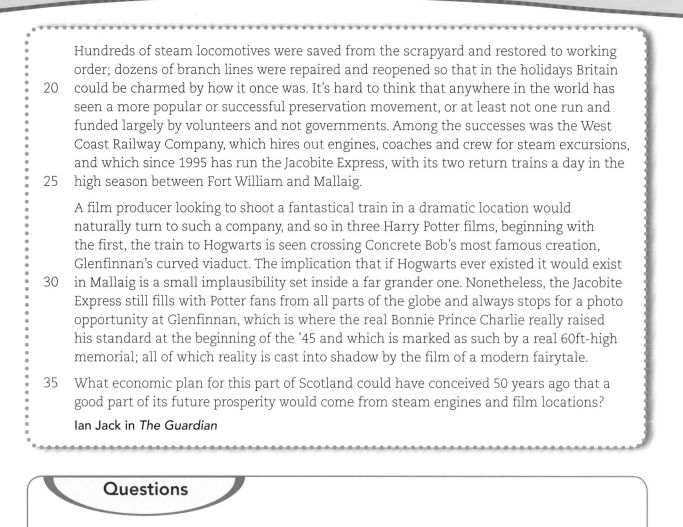

Hundreds of steam locomotives were saved from the scrapyard and restored to working order; dozens of branch lines were repaired and reopened so that in the holidays Britain

20 could be charmed by how it once was. It's hard to think that anywhere in the world has seen a more popular or successful preservation movement, or at least not one run and funded largely by volunteers and not governments. Among the successes was the West Coast Railway Company, which hires out engines, coaches and crew for steam excursions, and which since 1995 has run the Jacobite Express, with its two return trains a day in the

25 high season between Fort William and Mallaig.

A film producer looking to shoot a fantastical train in a dramatic location would naturally turn to such a company, and so in three Harry Potter films, beginning with the first, the train to Hogwarts is seen crossing Concrete Bob's most famous creation, Glenfinnan's curved viaduct. The implication that if Hogwarts ever existed it would exist

30 in Mallaig is a small implausibility set inside a far grander one. Nonetheless, the Jacobite Express still fills with Potter fans from all parts of the globe and always stops for a photo opportunity at Glenfinnan, which is where the real Bonnie Prince Charlie really raised his standard at the beginning of the '45 and which is marked as such by a real 60ft-high memorial; all of which reality is cast into shadow by the film of a modern fairytale.

35 What economic plan for this part of Scotland could have conceived 50 years ago that a good part of its future prosperity would come from steam engines and film locations?

Ian Jack in *The Guardian*

Questions

1. Identify nine facts from the first paragraph (lines 1–11) about the railway to Mallaig.
2. Of these, choose the four or five most important.
3. Re-read paragraph 3 (lines 18–25). What two activities enabled organisations such as the West Coast Railway Company to come into being?
4. From paragraph 4 (lines 26–34), identify three facts that are ignored in the face of the fictional Harry Potter.

Answers

Answers can be found at the end of Part One, on page 48.

SECTION 2 – EXPLANATION

Typical questions of this type begin:

Explain how the writer … or Explain what the writer …

This type of question is a step up in difficulty from simple identification. It requires you to show your understanding of complex ideas, to follow the writer's line of thought, or to understand her point of view.

- Context will help you with complex ideas.
- 'Signposts' will help with the line of thought.
- There are also little intensifying or modifying words that can affect your understanding of the writer's point of view.
- Anecdotes and examples will help with your overall understanding of a paragraph or passage.

Context

In the following sentences from the article 'Beyond a joke', **context** is key to your understanding.

Trying to explain a joke has long been considered an example of pedantic futility. That hasn't stopped academics and teachers through the ages from erecting vast and subtle theories of comedy that are ultimately useless.

Steven Poole in *The Guardian*

Task

Explain what, in the writer's view, is the outcome of 'trying to explain a joke'.

Answer

In order to answer this question you have to understand what 'pedantic futility' means. The context – in this case the sentence that follows the phrase – allows you to make a good guess, even if you didn't know the meaning of 'pedantic' or 'futility'.

Understanding 'futility' is easier, because you probably have some idea of what it means, and you can get the words 'ultimately useless' from the next sentence. The meaning of 'pedantic' therefore must come from something earlier in that sentence, that is from 'academics and teachers' – people who make claims to know the answers ('vast and subtle theories'). So the result of trying to explain a joke is a useless academic exercise leading nowhere.

Signposts

Signposts – such as 'but', 'although', 'because of', 'however' – can be useful in showing cause and effect, contradiction or contrast, among other things.

Here is another little extract from 'Beyond a joke':

What the author of the book does not offer, though, is any kind of reason why an 'Aha!' response to a problem is different from a 'Haha!' response to a joke. He tries to convince us using technical terminology, but the same technical terminology can be used to explain problem solving. So the effect of jokes is really not explained. We are obviously no closer to understanding why is it satisfying to solve a puzzle, but amusing to get a joke.

Task

Explain what criticisms the writer makes of the book.

Answer

The writer can't show any difference between the two responses to jokes and problems, so he has not helped us to understand what makes a joke funny.

In this case, useful signposts are 'but', 'So', 'Why … but …' These words tend to show the movement through the writer's line of thought.

Modifying or intensifying

There are also little words that have a **modifying or intensifying** function, and that can change a statement subtly to show what the writer is thinking. Words such as 'just', 'even' and 'clearly' are examples of these.

- 'He was **just** trying to be helpful' suggests that he was not, in fact, being much use.
- '**Even** the policeman believed his story' is stronger than 'The policeman believed his story'.

In the example above from 'Beyond a joke', 'though' and 'obviously' are clues to the writer's bias. Later on in the article there are other examples of words that signal his bias. These include:

1. 'We are invited to agree that …'
2. 'Another aspect of humour supposedly revealed by science …'
3. '[The scientist] claims that humour tends to target …'
4. 'Such moral questions about comedy are, of course, simply not answerable by neuroscientific explanations …'

Task

Explain how, in each of the four examples above, the writer shows his scepticism about a scientific explanation of humour.

Answers

1. 'We are invited to agree' suggests that the writer feels he is being lured (unjustifiably) into going along with what the scientist says.

2. 'supposedly' suggests that this aspect is not actually revealed – it is in the mind of only the scientist.

3. 'claims' suggests that the scientist is making a statement that he can't prove.

4. 'of course' shows the writer's view that only a fool would think that scientific explanations are true.

Examples and anecdotes

Examples and anecdotes don't usually form part of an explanation but they do reinforce your understanding of the points the writer is making. They illustrate the writer's argument in the same way that context can help you understand the meaning of individual words and phrases.

Further practice

The following exercise will illustrate several of the ideas above.

Sometimes it is right to wipe out a species

The World Health Organization's annual assembly, in the face of contrary advice from independent experts, decided recently not to set a date to destroy the last two remaining samples of smallpox virus kept in secure laboratories in Atlanta and Novosibirsk. Smallpox, being a virus, does not really count as a living species. But the prospect of the
5   deliberate extinction of some harmful species is getting closer. Be in no doubt – it would be an unambiguously good thing.

Unfortunately, the imminent eradication of the guinea worm in Africa has suffered a setback this year. Last month there were just three new cases, down from 25 last year and 80 the year before that, but one of them was in Chad in an area previously thought
10   to be free of the problem. Despite this, the parasite seems to be on the way to eradication.

Is such deliberate extinction of creatures that cause suffering a good idea? As long as the effect on the ecosystems is small, then the answer is clearly yes. Take mosquitoes, for example. There are 2500 species of mosquito in the world and only one of them – *Aedes aegyti* – is responsible for carrying dengue fever, a disease that currently afflicts
15   nearly 400 million people, a figure that is rising. If you were to wave a magic wand and get rid of *A aegyti*, then there would be plenty of other mosquitoes to take its place in ponds and puddles.

And waving such a magic wand is no longer completely implausible. Last month the Brazilian Government gave an Oxford-based company a licence to release into the wild
20   genetically engineered male *A aegyti* mosquitoes. They carry two extra genes that render their offspring incapable of breeding. Release enough of these mosquitoes into an area and the species all but dies out locally. The beauty of this scheme is that the rarer the species gets, the better are the chances that the genetically engineered males you release will mate with any available females, so the technique becomes more effective, not less,
25   as local extinction approaches.

→

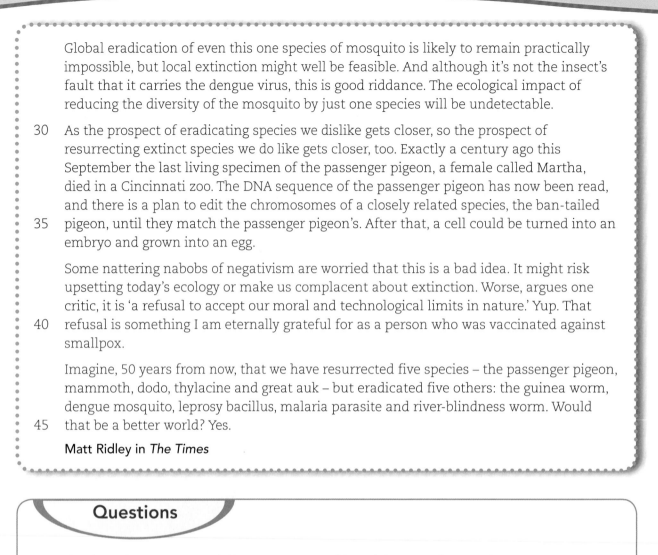

Global eradication of even this one species of mosquito is likely to remain practically impossible, but local extinction might well be feasible. And although it's not the insect's fault that it carries the dengue virus, this is good riddance. The ecological impact of reducing the diversity of the mosquito by just one species will be undetectable.

30   As the prospect of eradicating species we dislike gets closer, so the prospect of resurrecting extinct species we do like gets closer, too. Exactly a century ago this September the last living specimen of the passenger pigeon, a female called Martha, died in a Cincinnati zoo. The DNA sequence of the passenger pigeon has now been read, and there is a plan to edit the chromosomes of a closely related species, the ban-tailed
35   pigeon, until they match the passenger pigeon's. After that, a cell could be turned into an embryo and grown into an egg.

Some nattering nabobs of negativism are worried that this is a bad idea. It might risk upsetting today's ecology or make us complacent about extinction. Worse, argues one critic, it is 'a refusal to accept our moral and technological limits in nature.' Yup. That
40   refusal is something I am eternally grateful for as a person who was vaccinated against smallpox.

Imagine, 50 years from now, that we have resurrected five species – the passenger pigeon, mammoth, dodo, thylacine and great auk – but eradicated five others: the guinea worm, dengue mosquito, leprosy bacillus, malaria parasite and river-blindness worm. Would
45   that be a better world? Yes.

Matt Ridley in *The Times*

Questions

1. Explain how the writer views 'deliberate extinction of harmful species' (lines 1–6).
2. Explain how the writer's use of mosquitoes as an example backs his idea that deliberate extinction is allowable (lines 11–17).
3. Explain how such an extinction is becoming possible (lines 18–25).
4. Explain why the critics of resurrecting extinct species think it is a bad idea (lines 37–41).

Answers

Answers can be found at the end of Part One, on page 49.

Conclusion

Your understanding of the complex ideas of a passage can be deepened by looking at the context of unfamiliar words and phrases, by following the line of thought using signposts, repetition and climax, and by detecting bias on the part of the writer.

List of terms used

Context, signposts, modifiers or intensifiers, bias, point of view.

Hint

Some pointers to the bias of the writer can be found in his use of phrases such as 'Be in no doubt' (line 5), 'clearly' (line 12), 'even this one species' (line 26), and his repetition of 'yes' and 'yup' throughout – ending on a 'Yes'.

Supplementary passage

Heard the one about women on TV?

Not getting on the box means female comics don't earn the money to tour and hone their skills.

Women are under-represented in TV comedy for a variety of reasons, the hackneyed 'fear that women aren't funny' being one of them. Therefore, the fees available for being funny on television do not, broadly, go to women. So, aspirant female stand-ups do not have the money to support the tours they should do to sharpen their material and become better known.

5   It's hard enough to pay travel expenses for low-paid live club gigs, never mind touring a solo show or going to the Edinburgh Fringe, which is the very best place to hone, to practise and to garner attention. Edinburgh is the breeding ground for most of the celebrated comedians we know today.

Anyone who is currently packing for this year's Fringe will know the huge costs attached:
10   flat rental for the month; venue hire (which falls to the performers, who often discover they have made a loss even after a series of sell-out shows); advertising space in the programme; poster and flyer printing …

If women aren't getting TV fees, they either can't afford to tour or they must subsidise themselves with other jobs, which can prevent them from travelling

➡

15   anyway. Nor will they get a live audience easily if they haven't been on TV. It is, in a stroke of good news for fans of cliché, both a Catch-22 and a vicious circle. If they can't afford to practise their material and find a fan base beyond their home town, they won't get on to TV, so they won't be able to … well, you get the idea.

   You might say that the problem of not getting TV fees to support a new career would
20   apply to any aspiring comedian, but producers and bookers are much quicker to offer space to unknown men than to women. They do want to 'break new talent', and if an obscure male comic has a bad show then they will assume the problem either lies with him or an off night, not with his gender. A woman who gets no laughs, however, will appear to confirm a broader sweep of secret fears – 'that women can't be funny'.

25   I'm not unsympathetic; a television series is not a charity enterprise, and of course producers' first priority must be to make it funny. But how do they test what's funny? Gauging audience laughter is not reliable because audiences react best to what they know. It's not just producers who are sexist; crowds are too. With the best will in the world, they can feel nervous for female performers – and, with less goodwill, irritated
30   when they see women appearing to boss men around.

   This is a problem that will disappear as soon as female comics are a more common sight, but I'm afraid that the new policy of insisting on 'at least one per show' might not help. Too often, producers translate 'at least one per show' into 'one per show'. I'm not a comedian but I have been told straight by TV bookers, when giving my availability to
35   appear on something: 'We already have a woman for the 19th … Could you do the 26th?' All it would take is for one generation of broadcasters to take the plunge and aim for a 50/50 mix, using the dozens of female performers who are out there waiting for a break.

   Does it matter? Should they bother? It's only comedy, after all, not the House of Commons or the Supreme Committee for Educational Policy in Saudi Arabia. And yet I do
40   think it has importance.

   Television is where our national conversation is held. It's where opinions are aired and formed, jokes made and voices heard. Whether comedy, news debate, drama or documentary, if any gender, race, class or age group dominates out of all proportion to our true national mix, that conversation is weakened and our opinions misshapen as a
45   result. It is worth trying harder.

Victoria Coren Mitchell in *The Observer*

Questions

1. Explain why female comedians are disadvantaged by today's TV set-up (lines 1–4).
2. Explain the 'Catch-22' and/or the 'vicious circle' referred to in lines 13–18.
3. Re-read lines 19–30. Explain how, even if a woman does get a chance, she still has to overcome problems that a male comic does not face.
4. Explain the disadvantage of the 'new policy' mentioned in line 32.
5. Explain why the writer thinks that, even though 'It's only comedy, after all' (line 38), it is very important for our society as a whole.

Answers

Answers can be found at the end of Part One, on pages 49–50.

SECTION 3 – ANALYSIS

This type of question usually asks for an analysis of some aspect of language. Typical questions begin:

Analyse how …

Four of the most important aspects of analysis are dealt with in this chapter:

- Word choice
- Imagery
- Sentence structure
- Tone

There are, of course, lots of other devices writers use to enliven their writing, and make it effective: typography, anecdote, rhyme, cadence, quotation, and so on.

All of the aspects above come under the heading of 'the writer's use of language' – any of which you might be asked to analyse.

Word choice

What is special about word choice in the way that it is identified for questioning in Higher English passages? It is surely obvious that all professional writers choose their words with care, so all words can be described as 'chosen'. By focusing on the use of particular words in particular contexts, however, you can see how you are being manipulated or entertained, or attracted or emotionally affected, by the writer's choice.

In **descriptive** passages, word choice might be a main method whereby the mood or atmosphere of a particular scene is conveyed. In **persuasive** passages, word choice might be one of the methods used to influence your ideas or predispose you to look favourably on the argument. In a piece of **comic writing**, the word choice will alert you to the tone and set up expectations for entertainment.

Given the nature of the kind of passages normally examined in Higher English papers, it is more than likely that the main focus will be on words that attempt to influence you by conveying ideas from the writer's point of view. There will also be occasions where a descriptive passage or a humorous tone is marked by interesting and emotive word choice.

Denotation and connotation

The effect of words on you, their ability to move you or persuade you, depends on their connotations. All words have a **denotation** – a direct definition or basic 'meaning':

- An infant, for example, is 'the young of the human species'.
- A baby is also 'the young of the human species'.
- So is a 'neonate' – except that this is a medical term.

The **connotations** of these words are, however, very different:

- 'Infant' is a sort of social description – it marks out a small member of the human race; one of us, but very young (in its original Latin derivation it means 'not speaking').

- 'Baby' is a much more personal description, suggesting affection, closeness, vulnerability.

- 'Neonate' is the medical description of a newly born child. It has connotations of classification and objectivity.

If the plight of these young beings in a refugee camp were being described, there might be three separate descriptions, which would have very different effects on you:

- 'Starving babies'

- 'Malnutrition among the infants'

- 'Neonatal death rate'

Task

In what kind of communication would you be likely to find each of these descriptions, and what is the effect of each?

Answer

You would expect to find 'starving babies' in an article seeking to bring the plight of these babies to the notice of the public in such a way as to make the reader feel sorry for them.

You would expect to find mention of 'infant mortality' in a report for an organisation or institution that collects information about famines – 'the infants' suggests that this group is vulnerable to hunger.

You would expect to find 'neonatal death rate' in a list of medical statistics – 'neonatal' suggesting something almost scientific. This is rather distancing in terms of human emotion.

Persuasive

Often the words a writer uses are biased or 'loaded' in such a way as to push you into accepting his or her point of view. In the following passage the writer is making a persuasive case for not overusing the resources of the NHS, but he is combining his argument with humour, presumably to entertain the reader and keep him or her reading to the end.

Doctor, I feel slightly funny

The nation is healthier than ever, yet the NHS is permanently struggling to cope. The writer explains why patients, politicians and drug companies have a lot to answer for.

There's a theory that the real problem with the NHS is not too few doctors, but too many patients. Some politicians like to pin it on the fact that we've become a nation of accident-prone, alcoholic, smoking lard-buckets. If only we could all learn to eat, drink and be merry responsibly, then half the health budget wouldn't be frittered away on
5   potentially preventable diseases. Sociologists prefer to blame the politicians for creating mass involuntary euthanasia in the UK. It's called living in the North of England. The rich live 10 years longer than the poor – and the gap is widening. Until it narrows, no health service will ever cope.

10 An additional strain on the NHS is that it is full of patients who have little to gain from being there. The beauty of the NHS – that you can be scraped off the pavement without having to check for your Barclaycard – is also its weakness. Any service that is free at the front door encourages life's little problems to become medicalised. A GP friend was phoned at 3 a.m. by the relative of a man marching drunk down the high street with his glass eye balanced on the end of his nose. It's a fine trick, and worthy of an audience, but

15 it doesn't require a doctor.

Another GP has a T-shirt with 'CAMERA' on it: the Campaign for Real Ailments. Much of his workload consists of defusing the anxiety of an increasingly 'worried-well' population who don't have any discernible disease, just an awareness of what might, or might not, be 'risk factors'. Alas, in the doomed pursuit of a risk-free life, their new health awareness

20 makes them pathologically anxious and they end up on antidepressants. Great for the drug industry, but not great medicine.

A column in *Pharmaceutical Marketing* recently emphasised the importance the industry attaches to shaping medical and public opinion: 'You may even need to reinforce the actual existence of a disease and/or the value of treating it. A classic example of this was

25 the need to create recognition in Europe of social phobia [another word for shyness] as a distinct clinical entity and the potential of antidepressants to treat it.' The suspicion here is that companies are creating drugs first and then finding diseases to match them to. Not so much a pill for every ill, but an ill for every pill.

It's easy to blame the drug industry, but they don't force us to medicalise our lives.

30 Every day, we swallow millions of pills of dubious benefit, because we like the colour or the name. Look at the range of tablets available over the counter – the exotic tinctures, linctuses, powders, pearls and salts. With most there's little evidence that they can out-perform a placebo, but we can't help ourselves. Or can we? Most prescription medicines fall into the rule of thirds. A third of patients take tablets properly, a third sporadically

35 and ineffectively, and a third either don't cash in the prescription or throw the tablets away. I was once accosted by an angry patient who claimed (rightly) that I had changed his tablets to a different brand. How did he know? Because the first lot sank when he threw them down the loo, and the new lot floated.

I'm 40 now and I haven't been to the GP for 22 years. I've no interest in finding out what

40 my blood pressure, cholesterol, body mass index or prostate are doing. I'm happy to take the risk. It's your choice, not the Health Minister's or your doctor's. The absurd paradox in medicine is that although we're living longer and healthier lives than ever, we're more concerned and anxious about our health. From an evolutionary perspective, we're just African apes on the briefest of joy rides. So let's enjoy it. If you feel well, you don't

45 have to let medicine screw it up. Death aside, most risks never happen and your body has an extraordinary capacity to survive life without doctors. Let's save the NHS for the genuinely sick.

Phil Hammond in *The Independent*

Questions

1. From lines 1–8, analyse how the word choice supports the idea that we overuse the NHS.

2. 'scraped off the pavement', 'life's little problems' (lines 10–12). What does the writer gain by his use of these words/phrases?

3. Analyse how the word choice in lines 16–21 suggests the negative aspects of the anxiety felt by people who are actually healthy.

4. Why would drug companies choose to call shyness 'social phobia' (line 25)?

5. Analyse how the writer's word choice in lines 29–38 describes his attitude to the pills people take.

Answers

Answers can be found at the end of Part One, on pages 50–51.

Conclusion

The effectiveness of word choice in a sentence or passage depends on your understanding of the connotational aspects of the word – what particular spin, bias or feeling is being suggested.

The larger your own vocabulary, the easier you will find it to explain the range of suggestions possible.

List of terms used

Connotation, writer's point of view, bias, persuasion, tone.

Supplementary exercise – Evocative/atmospheric

Although this book is about the Understanding, Analysis and Evaluation paper, many of the skills you are learning are transferrable to the questions on Scottish texts that you are asked about in Section 1 of the Critical Reading paper. Remember that you would not be given poetry to deal with in the Understanding, Analysis and Evaluation paper in the exam.

This next example is one of Norman MacCaig's poems. You would expect – because poetry is a very concentrated form of language – that there would be many opportunities to analyse word choice, and so it proves. In almost every line of the following poem, you could find a word that has been carefully chosen to create a feeling and an atmosphere, probably one of regret and loss.

'Sounds of the day'

When a clatter came,

it was horses crossing the ford.

When the air creaked, it was

a lapwing seeing us off the premises

5   of its private marsh. A snuffling puff

ten yards from the boat was the tide blocking and

unblocking a hole in a rock.

When the black drums rolled, it was water

falling sixty feet into itself.

10   When the door

scraped shut, it was the end

of all the sounds there are.

You left me

beside the quietest fire in the world.

15   I thought I was hurt in my pride only,

forgetting that,

when you plunge your hand in freezing water,

you feel

a bangle of ice round your wrist

20   before the whole hand goes numb.

Questions

1. Analyse the effect of words in the first verse that suggest particular sounds.
2. Still thinking of sounds, analyse the effect of 'scraped' (line 11).
3. What is the effect of the constant repetition of 'was' in the first two verses of the poem?
4. Evaluate the contribution of word choice to the effectiveness of the comparison between an ended relationship and putting a hand into cold water (lines 15–20).

Note

You would **not** be asked so many questions on word choice in Section 1 of the Critical Reading paper, but because we are dealing with word choice here, there are plenty of opportunities for you to apply your skill.

Answers

Answers can be found at the end of Part One, on pages 51–52.

Imagery

The discussion of imagery is the most interesting and most rewarding part of close reading. Close examination of imagery allows you to share the experience of the writer almost at first hand, making his thoughts your thoughts. A writer uses an image – **simile** or **metaphor** or **personification** – because he has seen or felt or been searching for a comparison that allows him to pass on to you his feelings and emotions at the immediate moment of experience. Imagery is a kind of shorthand that allows an experience to be transferred from the imagination of the writer to the imagination of the reader without necessarily going through a logical process. That's why it is 'magic' – in all senses of the word.

Look at the following paragraph from the book *Summit Fever* by Andrew Greig. In it he is describing the approaches to the high peaks of the Himalayas.

The scale of it all and the sheer desolation were a shock to the mind and body. It scooped us out of ourselves like the stars do. It left us feeling tiny and liberated, finally jolted us free from the shell of our supposed importance.

Here the writer is trying to convey how vast the emptiness of the mountains was and how small it made him feel. He uses a simile and a metaphor to try to convey that feeling to us:

The scale of it all and the sheer desolation … scooped us out of ourselves like the stars do.

… finally jolted us free from the shell of our supposed importance.

The first of these, the simile, is easier to unravel. He is saying that the scale and emptiness of the landscape is as vast and as empty as the stars and the space surrounding them, and that it has the same effect on him. So you are getting an impression of the cold and of the infinity of space surrounding and possibly overwhelming him.

But what is he getting at when he says 'scooped us out of ourselves'? Does it suggest it 'left us feeling hollow', as if our souls had been sucked out by the vastness of the space? Or it took our needs and desires away to leave only a love of the universe? These are possible ideas based on the literal meaning of 'scooped' – hollowed out.

Perhaps further clarification arrives with the metaphor of the 'shell'. 'Free from the shell of our supposed importance' suggests that our self-centred-ness interferes with our appreciation of the really important transcendent and infinite beauty/power/unknowableness of the universe, and that at moments such as he is describing the self can become unimportant, freed from its own limitations.

Remember that the basis for a metaphor is a statement that is not 'true'. Human beings do not have 'shells' in the literal sense. The combination of 'scoop' and 'shell' suggests literally that we can be freed from our limitations, as a sea creature can be flipped out of its shell, or perhaps even a bird being liberated from the prison of its shell.

There are other possible interpretations that will depend on the reader's sensitivity to the imagery the writer has used. Any appropriate interpretation involving the literal meaning of the 'image' words (the 'root', if you like) and their extension into the figurative or metaphorical ideas they spark off – space, cold, emptiness, freedom, infinity … – will be acceptable.

The exploration of imagery, in the case of metaphor/personification, usually requires 'seeing' which aspects or connotations of the literal meaning of the word or phrase are being shared with the figurative idea to help you to appreciate the comparison the writer is making. Or, in the case of a simile, identifying which aspects of the two 'sides' highlight the connotational area(s) they have in common.

The following extract is from another of Andrew Greig's books, *At the Loch of the Green Corrie*, in which he describes a fishing trip to the loch in Assynt, north-west Scotland, which the poet Norman MacCaig said was his favourite place on earth.

At the Loch of the Green Corrie

I've never fished from here before, at the southern end of the corrie. Towering at my back, the scree curtain wraps round two-thirds of the lochan. The open aspect is now on my right, where the land falls away into the distance. From here this lochan is not so much hidden in a hollow as reclining on a high balcony. And the water, which from the other
5   shore impatiently swatted away the light, has become transparent. I am looking right through the water's surface to long wavering tendrils of green ropes of weed. Among them, something brown and plump wanders lazily, its mouth pouting … I blink. It's gone.

So it's true, there are grand fish in here. That one had to be well over three pounds. Maybe Ewan MacCaig was right when he suggested that his father valued this place simply because
10   it had big, fat brown trout. Yet as I urgently cast and retrieve and cast again around the place where I saw that fish, I reject that explanation. It's far too reductionist. MacCaig was not a reductionist. When his noticing eye fell on a landscape, a loch, a friend, a collie, a tattered rose bush, his heart would give them their true size and value. In the end his poetry is not so much a matter of words as a function of a noticing eye, the opening heart, the balancing mind.

15   I cast again out towards the flicker. Even as this fresh cast snags the ruffled surface, I am sure: Norman MacCaig loved the Loch of the Green Corrie as the essence of Assynt because of its removal from the world, because of the austerity and difficulty that enhance the place's nature, and on account of certain friends who once stood by him here.

The wind shifts and a flying hook embeds in my hat. I force it out then walk back round
20   to the little northern promontory. This is where we first came in. This is where, in one way or another, it will end. My arm aches, sun has gone, wind is cold. My casts are slowing. I'm a clockwork fisherman running down.

Just as I left Edinburgh a friend said 'Going for a few days' escapism?' It niggles still, that remark, even as I finally get my line out again, facing the bleak screescape with the light
25   breeze behind. Everything is clear and sharp now – the travelling slash of ripples, cool breeze over my hands, my own roughened skin, smell of turf and heather. I've escaped not from life but out into it.

We see the effects of wind, the things caught up in it, not the wind itself. I watch the far side of the corrie lose colour, then that end of the lochan darken, become riddled with grey. A pale
30   spiral swirls and flattens, coming this way. A rattling sound, then in a drenching blow the hail squall hits. Shoes filling, trousers sodden, fingers turning white in the wet half-gale – it's clear I'm finished here. That big fish I glimpsed, almost insolent in its nonchalance, is long gone.

Chittering with cold, stepping carefully across the growling burn, a hunchback under my sodden backpack, I hurry down through the storm.

In this descriptive passage Greig is obviously using all the literary weapons he has available. He uses carefully chosen words and many similes and metaphors. He has obviously found the Assynt landscape both evocative of his friend Norman MacCaig, and of a singular strange beauty. He wants to convey to us the feelings he has had there, so that we can share in his fascination and sense of remembrance.

Questions

1. In the first paragraph (lines 1–7) there are two metaphors, a simile and a personification:
   'the scree curtain'
   'as reclining on a … balcony'
   'impatiently swatted away'
   'green ropes'
   Analyse how each of these images is effective in giving a clarity to the writer's description of the lochan.
2. Identify one metaphor in the third paragraph (lines 15–18) and one in the fourth paragraph (lines 19–22). Analyse the effect of each. Which seems to you to be the more effective?
3. Re-read lines 23–32. Consider the phrases 'bleak screescape', 'the travelling slash of ripples', 'become riddled with grey'. It would be possible to comment on these phrases either as imagery or as word choice. Choose one of the three phrases, and comment on both aspects.
4. Analyse how the imagery of the last paragraph (lines 33–34) paints an uncomfortable picture. You should deal with both personification and metaphor.

Answers

Answers can be found at the end of Part One, on pages 52–53.

Conclusion

In each kind of image – metaphor, simile, personification – there is at its heart a comparison: the writer has used two related ideas that, together, help you to see, understand or feel what the writer has seen, understood or felt. At its best, imagery gives the reader a new, fresh, striking insight into the subject.

List of terms used

Simile, metaphor, personification, comparison, literal, figurative, denotation, connotation.

Supplementary exercise

Although this book is about the Understanding, Analysis and Evaluation paper in the exam, many of the skills you are learning are transferrable to the questions on Scottish texts that you are asked about in Section 1 of the Critical Reading paper.

The extract below is from the beginning of Iain Crichton Smith's short story 'The Telegram'.

The Telegram

The two women – one fat and one thin – sat at the window of the thin woman's house drinking tea and looking down the road that ran through the village. They were like two birds, one a fat domestic bird perhaps, the other more aquiline, more gaunt, or to be precise, more like a buzzard.

5   It was wartime and although the village appeared quiet, much had gone on in it. Reverberations from a war fought far away had reached it: many of its young men had been killed, or rather drowned, since nearly all of them had joined the navy, and their ships had sunk in seas that they had never seen except on maps hung on the walls of the local school that they had all at one time or another unwillingly attended. One had been

10   drowned on a destroyer after a leave during which he had told his family that he would never come back again. (Or at least that was the rumour in the village, which was still, as it always had been, a superstitious place.) Another had been drowned during the pursuit of the *Bismarck*.

What the war had to do with them the people of the village did not know. It came on

15   them as a strange plague, taking their sons away and then killing them, meaninglessly, randomly. They watched the road often for the telegrams.

The telegrams were brought to the houses by the local elder who, clad in black, would walk along the road and then stop at the house to which the telegram was directed. People began to think of the telegram as a strange missile pointed at them from

20   abroad. They did not know what to associate it with, certainly not with God, but it was a weapon of some kind, it picked a door and entered it, and left desolation just like any other weapon.

Questions

1. Analyse the effectiveness of the imagery in paragraph 1 (lines 1–4) in introducing the two main characters in the story.
2. In paragraph 3 (lines 14–16) analyse how the imagery adds to our understanding of the effects of the war.
3. Analyse how the extended image in the last paragraph (lines 17–22) emphasises the fear created by the telegrams.

Answers

Answers can be found at the end of Part One, on page 53.

Sentence structure

Sentences are the basic building blocks of our communication. They put words in sequences which make sense and communicate, for example, an instruction or an idea or a question. Their shape can increase your understanding, your enjoyment and appreciation. The understanding of the effect of sentence structure is hard to explain. Most people can see that there are tricks the writer has used to affect the way we read, but it is difficult to express how these tricks work. You can identify a number of signals that something special is happening: short sentences; repetition of a clause, phrase, word or sound; parallelism of structure, balance, antithesis; use of lists; climax; obvious punctuation; links … Merely identifying the use of these features, however, will profit you nothing: you have to make a comment about their effect in context.

The following article illustrates a number of these aspects.

Bilingualism is good for you

Learning another language is wonderful. You may not completely buy the Sapir-Whorf hypothesis – the deliciously sci-fi name given by linguists to the idea that the words we use determine the thoughts we think. But knowing that the French have 'fat mornings' instead of lie-ins, or that in Farsi the part of you that gets broken is not the heart but
5 the gut, gives you a level of insight into the modes and mores of a culture that it is impossible to get by any other means.

Scientists tell us that learning a language is good for our brains, too. Evidence presented this week in the *Annals of Neurology* suggests that speaking more than one language improves cognition. Schoolchildren should be encouraged to become as bilingual as they
10 can possibly be.

I heartily agree. Children raised with two languages are lucky indeed, but for the rest of us, the very fact of being monolingual can be a spur to intellectual discovery, so long as you're at least exposed to the idea of other languages. I believed there were so many languages in the world that simply by babbling nonsense I would end up saying
15 something meaningful in one of them.

That last experiment must have been inspired by my dad, who, being Iranian, was often found on the end of the phone making bizarre noises into the receiver. Over the years, my siblings and I learned to recognise a few words. *Tarjimmykonee* was one, *azbezutumkay* another. We repeated them like magical incantations; but they meant as much to us
20 as 'abracadabra' did. But we knew they stood for something, and they felt all the more powerful for it.

When I found out what these phrases actually were, I realised how far our English ears had distorted them: *tavajoh mikonee* literally means 'Are you paying attention?' – perhaps better translated as 'Do you follow?'; *Arz be hozuretan ke* means, delightfully, 'a petition to
25 your presence that …' – a very formal, old fashioned phrase that amounts to 'If I could just say …'

30   As I got older, I grew increasingly frustrated that this world of knowledge had been
      denied to me. I knew that parents had the power to transmit language to their children;
      it seemed to come down naturally through the generations, like hair colour or the
      shape of your nose. But I had missed out. 'Why didn't you teach us Farsi?' I complained.
      The answers – 'I didn't have time' and 'Your mother didn't speak it' – seemed feeble
      then but are understandable in retrospect: he was working full time, in a completely
      English environment, knowing that I would have no one to practise with when he wasn't
      there. No one talks about a 'father tongue', after all.

35   When I was 12 or 13, I tried to learn Farsi on my own, kitting myself out with the whole works:
      cassettes, dictionary, phrase book, exercise book, and a large stock of chocolate. I crawled
      part of the way through the strange new alphabet but didn't have the discipline – who would,
      at that age, with no classmates, no teacher, no one to get into trouble with for unfinished
      homework? When I got to university I decided there was only one option. If I was locked into
40   a regime of daily lectures, grammar exercises and conversation classes, with the prospect of
      some very difficult exams at the end of it, then I would probably, finally, manage it. I stopped
      studying history, switched department and embarked on a degree in Arabic and Persian.

      The next three years were completely fascinating, though not always plain sailing. But
      what I learned was that the 'sensitive period' for the acquisition of language had long
45   passed. I would never be bilingual, much less pass for a native speaker. My fascination
      with the way that languages worked – driven by that feeling of being locked out of my
      dad's verbal world – grew into a love of linguistics.

      So even if the bilingualism prize remains out of reach, the study of language has hugely
      enriched my life. I can only echo the comments: if you have the opportunity to learn – or,
50   better still, to pass on – a language, then grab it with both hands.

David Shariatmadari in *The Guardian*

Some of the aspects illustrated in this extract are:

Short sentence

The very first sentence of this article – 'Learning another language is wonderful.' – is short, but what is the effect of this? It could be described as a declarative sentence – in other words it is supremely confident and is giving a very positive start to the article. It is also an important statement of the topic of the whole article, and suggests that everything that follows will enthusiastically deal with the subject of bilingualism.

Short sentences can be described in many other ways – dramatic, summative or contradictory, for example.

Climax

'My fascination … grew into a love of linguistics' (lines 45–47). This climax to the paragraph is effective as it brings the reader back to one of the positive aspects of learning a language – the emotional kick the writer gets out of it.

Punctuation

Punctuation has, as its primary function, the power to lead us through a sentence in such a way that we 'get' the meaning. An example of this is:

The answers – 'I didn't have time' and 'Your mother didn't speak it' – seemed feeble then but are understandable in retrospect: he was working full time, in a completely English environment, knowing that I would have no one to practise with when he wasn't there.

The two dashes signal a parenthesis within which the writer enlarges on the idea of the 'answers' that seemed to him feeble.

The inverted commas obviously tell us that these were his father's words, and possibly indicate that these words were often repeated.

Note

One dash does not signal a parenthesis; there have to be two items – either dashes, commas or brackets – to mark off the parenthetical phrase.

The colon prepares us for an explanation of why the writer now feels that these excuses were 'understandable' – the explanation being about lack of time, lack of a Farsi environment, lack of people to practise with. In the explanation, commas are used to help isolate each of the reasons for his father's refusal.

Now it's over to you to answer the following questions on the extract.

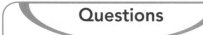

Questions

1. What is the function of the dash in line 2?
2. What are two possible functions of the short sentence in line 11?
3. 'We repeated them like magical incantations; but they meant as much to us as "abracadabra" did.' (lines 19–20)
   Analyse how the sentence structure adds to your understanding of the children's ignorance of Farsi.
4. Analyse how the punctuation helps to clarify the meaning of the sentence 'When I found out …' to 'If I could just say …' (lines 22–26).
5. Re-read lines 35–39 ('When I was … homework').
   Identify and analyse two aspects of sentence structure in these lines that help the reader understand the struggles of the writer to learn Farsi.
6. Analyse how the sentence structure in the last paragraph (lines 48–50) helps to bring the article to a satisfactory conclusion.

Questions 1 and 2 are much narrower and more restrictive than questions you will face in the exam paper, but they give you practice in learning how to incorporate aspects of sentence structure into a longer answer to a wider question.

Answers

Answers can be found at the end of Part One, on pages 53–54.

Conclusion

You should have a list of items which you can explore to see what aspect of structure is being deployed effectively by the writer.

Such aspects might be:

- the use of short sentences
- repetition of clause, phrase, word or sound
- parallelism of structure, balance, antithesis
- use of lists
- links in argument
- climax, anti-climax
- punctuation (and you should have a supplementary list of different punctuation functions).

List of terms used

All the important words you have learned about in this section are in the list above.

Supplementary exercise

A seatbelt that stops me dozing off at the wheel? Baaa humbug to that

The perception of risk from an old fashioned act of butchery, to the risks of a new design in seatbelts.

The other day, I had an old fashioned experience: I bought some lamb chops at a butcher's shop. It wasn't just that it was a slightly old fashioned sort of food – a basis for a meal that's been around as long as I can remember, when spaghetti came only as bolognese or hoops, and pizzas were saucer-sized frozen frisbees in all the yellows and
5   brick reds of a festering wound.

And it wasn't just that I was buying it in an old fashioned way – from an actual butcher's shop, which basically sells only meat. I have to admit, though, they're cheating slightly by also having a cheese counter and a range of chutneys. But they're not cheating massively, as they would by also having an out-of-town location, a vast car park, a section for every

10   other sort of food, as well as clothes, books, bank accounts, insurance, toys, inflatable swimming pool accessories, and probably actual houses.

The aspect of the encounter I thought was most old fashioned was that the butcher had to cut the chops from a larger piece of meat. I enjoyed watching this non-metaphorical act of butchery. Not because I delight in the dismembering of an adorable infant sheep,

15   but because of the bladework. Using a large dull steel knife, which turned out to be the sharpest grey thing since Alistair Darling's hairdo, and occasionally aided by a swift clip of the cleaver, the butcher efficiently transformed the meat into chops without removing even one of his fingers. And his fingers, let's not forget, are basically made out of the same thing as the lamb.

20   This process felt entirely safe, even though it was obviously dangerous. It didn't happen slowly and nervously, like the defusing of a bomb. It was matter-of-fact and quick. He knew he wasn't going to cut his fingers off and he didn't. It felt old fashioned watching something potentially hazardous happen without it being surrounded by the paraphernalia of risk limitation: he didn't have to put on a mask or gloves, set a trip

25   alarm that would go off if his skin was pierced, take a prophylactic dose of antibiotics, put the local A&E on standby, or hand me a splatter shield. He just knew what he was doing.

I needed this breath of historical air because I'd just read about Harken. Harken is a new sort of seatbelt, being developed by some Spanish and Portuguese scientists, that is designed to spot whether you might be dozing off behind the wheel and to wake you up if

30   you are. The hope is that such devices will avert some of the 20 per cent of road accidents thought to be caused by tiredness.

I know that, at first glance, this sounds like an incontrovertibly good idea; but, on consideration, it's a bad idea that I don't like at all. For one thing, these systems will definitely go wrong in ways that are incredibly annoying. Harken is supposed to monitor

35   the modifications of breathing and heart rate that predate the first signs of fatigue or drowsiness, and therefore to warn the driver before the symptoms of tiredness appear. So it knows you're feeling drowsy before you do. Anyone who has followed developments in car technology – who grasps that the primary function of an electric window is to break down when it's open, and that car alarms serve purely to wake up neighbours

40   and alert distant thieves to the presence of an expensive vehicle – will realise that these contraptions are going to go off all the time.

But even if they work properly, which I suppose they probably will after 10 years of irritation, they're an ominous development. Driving a car, like chopping meat with a cleaver, is a risky business. Awareness of that risk, and the skills and care it engenders,

45   are what makes the process statistically safe: there is an onus on the driver to be competent. So, for God's sake, let's not have people who think they might fall asleep at the wheel getting behind it anyway because there's a machine that they reckon makes it OK. That's the sort of safety net on which people get garrotted. Giving an exhausted human the illusion of consequence-free power strikes me as a perverse approach to

50   reducing road deaths.

David Mitchell in *The Observer*

Questions

1. Analyse how the sentence structure in the first paragraph (lines 1–5) helps to make an effective beginning for the article. (You should be looking for at least two aspects.)
2. What is the function of the first sentence in paragraph 2 (lines 6–7)?
3. How does the sentence structure of the second paragraph (lines 6–11) help to emphasise the difference between cheating 'slightly' and cheating 'massively'?
4. What two functions are fulfilled by the last sentence in paragraph 3 (lines 18–19)?
5. How is the idea of the modern obsession with risk emphasised by the sentence structure of lines 22–26 ('It felt … he was doing')?
6. Re-read paragraph 6 (lines 32–41).
   Choose two sentences in which the punctuation helps to clarify the meaning. Analyse the effect of the punctuation.

Answers

Answers can be found at the end of Part One, on pages 54–55.

Tone

Tone is a tricky concept to deal with in an analysis question. It is not a technique or a feature, as such. Tone is created by various techniques – structure, word choice, sound, point of view, juxtaposition, imagery, exaggeration, register …

Structure

Take the beginning of the article about our dependence on instant communication (see page 30):

Look at you with your CrackBerries and your iMgluedtomyphones. Addicted, I tell you. Addicted.

In this case, the structure of these sentences has a distinctly scathing tone. We, the readers, are in for a beating up. We are being addressed personally – 'you', 'your' and, strongest, 'I tell you'. The repetition of 'Addicted', and the one-word sentence 'Addicted.' make very clear what the writer thinks is wrong with us; but we can also tell from the word choice of 'CrackBerries' and 'iMgluedtomyphones' that he is making fun of us and our habits. So we know, right from the beginning, that the article is not straight or serious. It is more likely to try to get us to laugh at ourselves and thus become a little more self-aware, perhaps.

Word choice

An example of word choice suggesting tone is at the end of the article on bilingualism on pages 22–23. The last phrase – 'grab it with both hands' – concludes the enthusiastic tone that has been evident throughout.

Sound

The devices related to sound are rhyme, rhythm, repetition (of words, sounds or phrases), assonance and alliteration (which both also depend on repetition of a particular kind). There are others, but these are the more common ones.

It is not enough merely to identify, for example, alliteration. There also has to be comment on how the alliteration affects the impact, tone or mood of the communication.

In the following extract from an article on how children's toys have become less cuddly/friendly and more aggressive, alliteration is used to emphasise a rather disbelieving, tongue-in-cheek tone.

I suspect that the faces on Lego men and women have become grimmer because children keep pulling the heads off. I fear further that the news about Lego may be just the tip of the iceberg.

Has Barbie been overdoing the botox? How many designer scars does boyfriend Ken need? Not to mention that 'love/hate' tattoo on his knuckles and the builder's bum.

What other toys have been causing trauma? How many children have had an eye out in violent games of Tiddlywinks? Have snakes been getting longer and more vicious while ladders get shorter and shooglier? How many children have choked on the plastic triangles in Trivial Pursuit, thinking they are actually slices of cake?

Tom Shields in *The Herald*

The alliteration of the 'b' in 'Barbie' and 'botox' draws attention to the rather ludicrous idea of a plastic doll getting plastic surgery. This creates a tone of humorous disbelief.

Similarly, in 'ladders get shorter and shooglier' the alliteration puts some extra emphasis on the word 'shooglier', drawing attention to its register – dialectal rather than formal – which again suggests a lack of serious acceptance of the whole theory about modern toys. (Register is discussed below.)

Point of view (or writer's stance)

This is the angle from which a writer personally approaches the subject. If you look back to the article on pages 25–26, the writer is taking a position that is opposed to the idea of the new seatbelt.

He uses a particular tone – sarcasm or irony – to make us see his point of view. This is particularly obvious in the parenthesis in lines 38–40 – 'who … vehicle –'. Here he uses various sweeping statements about the unreliability of car gadgets to make his point about the dubious safety of a 'wake up' seatbelt.

Juxtaposition

This simply means deliberately putting together two words or concepts that seem to be in some way incongruous or opposed to each other. The effect of this can be to make you think again, or it can make you laugh.

In this short extract from an article called 'Car trips are bad trips' (see pages 34–35), the writer uses juxtaposition to underline his conviction that modern day car travel is a nightmare.

The only rational response to traffic conditions is hysteria. Last night I met a successful businesswoman (my wife) who had been moved to hopeless tears of frustration by the barbaric tussle of driving a mere three miles in central London.

The juxtaposition here of 'successful businesswoman' and '(my wife)' shows that presumably sensible, level-headed women who manage capably in the world of work, are rendered hysterical by the traffic. The incongruity of the juxtaposition is humorous, because we go from the exalted or high status term 'successful businesswoman' to the more mundane and intimate 'my wife'.

The article on female comedians on pages 11–12 juxtaposes television comedy with supposedly more important institutions: 'It's only [television] comedy, after all, not the House of Commons or the Supreme Committee for Educational Policy in Saudi Arabia.' But then the writer goes on to make the point that perhaps these eminent institutions are not as important for the ordinary man in the street as television is. This adds to the persuasive tone of the article.

Imagery

The whole tone in the last paragraph of the article on page 26 is pseudo-reasonable, conspiratorial, inviting you to be on the writer's side in the argument – he's just an ordinary bloke, after all.

So, for God's sake, let's not have people who think they might fall asleep at the wheel getting behind it anyway because there's a machine that they reckon makes it OK. That's the sort of safety net on which people get garrotted.

The colloquial nature of the language – 'for God's sake', 'they reckon makes it OK' – adds to this impression, and the image 'That's the sort of safety net on which people get garrotted' is deliberately chosen as a rather incongruous and exaggerated picture of someone fankled up in what is supposed to be saving them, but which is in fact strangling them – it's a sort of comic book image, not deadly serious.

Exaggeration

In the following extract from 'Car trips are bad trips' (see pages 34–35), the deliberate complexity of the vocabulary should tell you that there is something going on in the area of tone.

One-third of drivers never drive for pleasure and the rest do so only occasionally. Suffocating legislation and predatory local authorities threaten to criminalise even the saintliest individual suddenly possessed by the anti-social chutzpah required to drive a car. The only rational responses to confiscatory tickets and invasive speed cameras are intense spasmodic psychomotor agitation or harrowing paranoia.

The result of all the problems facing motorists is being blown out of proportion here for the biased purposes of the article. Exaggeration is at work, helping to create a highly negative, combative tone.

Register

This means using language appropriate to the situation. For example, in a formal situation, a job interview for instance, or in a serious newspaper article, it would not be considered appropriate to use a lot of slang vocabulary and colloquial phrases. These aspects of language would, however, be perfectly appropriate at a party with friends. The register chosen contributes to the tone of the communication.

Consider an example from the article on mosquitoes on page 10:

Worse, argues one critic, it is 'a refusal to accept our moral and technological limits in nature.' Yup. That refusal is something I am eternally grateful for as a person who was vaccinated against smallpox.

The writer uses the word 'Yup'. This is a colloquialism that you would not expect to find in a scientific article, but he is using it to add to the practical tone of his article – that he is just an ordinary chap who doesn't need to pay attention to the theorists and moralisers, and that he is just like us – the ordinary reader.

To return to the subject of the exercise – our discussion of tone.

The first necessity is to notice that a particular tone has been adopted. If the passages were read out to you in an appropriate tone, you would have no difficulty in recognising what was happening. That is because tone is created by 'voice' – you 'hear' the language as if someone were speaking it.

The words you use to identify tone are all words to do with speaking in a particular way. Words such as angry, wheedling, moaning, critical, humorous, doom-laden, hectoring and ironic could all describe a particular voice. Or as we have seen above: scathing, less than serious, disbelieving, tongue-in-cheek, biased, persuasive, reasonable, conspiratorial, combative, practical, down-to-earth.

If you are asked a question about tone, or if tone is suggested as one of the aspects of language you might look at in a question, then you can be fairly sure that there will be an obvious and identifiable tone. But you have to do more than just identify it. You have to show what alerted you to the tone – which words particularly suggested the tone you have identified. And you're still not finished: you have to relate the words you have chosen to the tone you have identified to show how they are linked.

Further practice

Out of office reply: I'm on hols but please keep me up to speed

Look at you with your CrackBerries and your iMgluedtomyphones. Addicted, I tell you. Addicted. It's got so bad that one in five young adults now admits they have checked their phones while snogging.

Our response to this shocking digital affliction divides neatly into national stereotypes. In
5   France, home of the 35-hour working week, one of the largest unions recently announced that its 250,000 members had 'an obligation to disconnect from communication tools of an evening'. The cheese-eating, work-shy surrender monkeys.

Then there are the Germans. Last week the car maker Daimler took a rather Teutonic approach to the horror of the holiday email backlog. Now, when its employees are away, any
10   emails they receive are deleted. Their out-of-office replies say something like: 'I am away. Your email has been deleted. If it was important, please contact my colleague instead.' Which translates as: 'I am busy bagsying sun loungers. Bother someone else instead. Danke schön.'

Imagine that. Coming back from holiday not to 327 health-and-safety updates and 12 messages from Geoff trying to sell his football tickets, but to nothing at all. Miraculously,
15   Daimler has not ground to a halt in the process. It is still managing to make cars. It appears that life goes on without holiday emails.

In Britain, where it is now impossible to hold a conversation with anyone for more than five minutes without them reaching for their phone (or is it just me?), we have the digital detox. This diet *du jour* comprises a cyber-blackout.

20   'Don't Facebook me this week,' people announce, as if preparing a mission to the dark side of the Moon. 'I'm on a digital detox. Wish me luck.'

The internet now offers tools to help cut time spent on the internet. For example, a man who was no longer engaging with his fiancée has designed an app called Moment, which sets daily online time limits. If you exceed them, it gives you an electric shock. (Well, it
25   doesn't, but it should.)

In the interests of proper research, I tried to buy this app. Spent 20 minutes surfing app stores to no avail and ended up downloading a game in which you must get a squiggly line into a series of ever-decreasing holes. Lost a whole afternoon to it.

Do we need a digital detox? Or Gallic regulation? Or Germanic email annihilation? Cast
30   your minds back to a time when phones were for making phone calls and you had to be at an actual desk with actual dial-up to check your actual email. Holidays were fine for the first couple of days but then came the fear, the dread, the lurking beast of paranoia.

What was happening back at work? Had Keith remembered to do that spreadsheet? Had Sandra done that thing Sandra was supposed to do? There's only one thing worse than
35   knowing what's gone wrong at work – and that's *not* knowing.

Now, with a click and a swipe and a few grand on roaming charges, I can nip all work horror in the bud from the comfort of that sun lounger.

You don't need a digital detox. You just need to stop checking your email when you're snogging. Are you listening to me? No, you're back on Facebook. Fine.

Matt Rudd in *The Times*

As we have already noted on page 27, the start of this article very quickly signals that its tone is not serious – it is pretending to be scathing, but gently so.

Questions

1. What would you identify as the tone of 'shocking digital affliction' (line 4)? How does it achieve its effect?
2. In lines 4–7, what factual point is made about the French reaction to digital overload and how does the writer undercut this by using stereotyping?
3. In lines 8–12, how does he adopt the same approach with the Germans?
4. Explain how he stereotypes the British in lines 13–16.
5. Re-read lines 17–21. What contribution does imagery make to the tone of the article?
6. How does the use of parenthesis in lines 24–25 sustain the tone he has adopted?
7. What is the contribution of the anecdote in lines 26–28 to the overall tone of the passage?
8. How do the content and structure of the last three sentences (line 39) make an effective end to the article?

> ### Note
> These questions are unlike questions you would get in the actual exam paper; they are designed just to concentrate your mind on the idea of 'tone'.

Answers

Answers can be found at the end of Part One, on pages 56–57.

Conclusion

Tone is not a simple feature of language; tone is created by other aspects of language, such as word choice, imagery, sentence structure, exaggeration and/or register. What you have to do when talking about tone is threefold:

1. Identify the tone you feel is being created.
2. Quote the words or structures that led you to your identification.
3. Link your quoted words, and so on, with the tone you have identified.

You may find that stages 2 and 3 can be fused together; that your comment is implicit in your choice of quotation.

Be particularly alert to the possibility that the tone adopted by the writer is ironic, mocking, tongue-in-cheek, sarcastic, and so on, as this means that statements cannot all be taken as straightforwardly 'true'.

List of terms used

Exaggeration, register, juxtaposition, incongruity, voice, sound.

Supplementary exercise

Commonwealth Games

Last week's *Last Week Tonight*, or maybe it was the week before's *Last Week Tonight* … anyway, at some time in the historical present, John Oliver did a comic bit attempting to explain the Commonwealth Games to Americans. It was a bit like a Bob Newhart sketch.*

5 'So, Walt, this is a club of people who were invaded, imprisoned, raped, robbed, enslaved, exploited and patronised by the limeys, in countries that were made up to suit Europeans, and they all get together every so often to play games? Really, Walt, and where do they do it? Glasgow? This is a club composed almost entirely of honeymoon destinations, and they make them do it in Glasgow? Did it rain, Walt? No, that was a rhetorical question. It's August, it's Scotland, of course it rained.'

10 The Commonwealth Games is a sports competition for 71 countries that were mostly so small, uncompetitive and underdeveloped that they could be taken over by a wooden gunboat and 20 Highlanders with dysentery. And so the British invite them back in order to beat them at games for which the British write the rules. Didn't you find the jingoism, the jockism, the unrelenting national congratulation, just the teeniest bit embarrassing?

15 We set up a sports meet that excludes America, China, Russia, Germany and France – all of which at some point we occupied – and behave as if we've just beaten the world. You'd imagine there were only five countries in the Commonwealth: England, Scotland, Wales, Australia and Canada. We insist the other small gamely developing nations come to Glasgow so that the fifth biggest economy in the world can beat them at cycling and

20 diving. Seen from outside, let me tell you, nothing about the Commonwealth Games makes us look good. We should be on our knees in gratitude that any of these people still want to talk to us. And if we are going to have a Commonwealth, couldn't we make it a bit more about them and a little less about us? We look like the fat rich kid with all the toys who always has to win because it's his garden.

25   One of the good things about the Commonwealth Games is that it's the sports that old people like: gently exciting, without raising the blood pressure. You can support your country and the places you went to on holiday or the ones that sent us bananas after the war; it's not obsessive, like football, and it isn't used to sell running shoes and fizzy drinks. It hasn't been bought up by satellite channels and it isn't cynical or violent. And

30   you get that nice Clare Balding.

* American comedian Bob Newhart's sketch on Sir Walter Raleigh and the discovery of tobacco can be found on YouTube.

A. A. Gill in *The Sunday Times*

Questions

1. Analyse how the opening paragraph (lines 1–3) sets up a less than serious tone.
2. Take each of the questions that 'Walt' is asked and analyse how the word choice or sentence structure creates a tone of mock disbelief.
3. In lines 10–24 the writer is critical of the home nations of the Commonwealth. By referring to two examples of his use of language, analyse how this critical tone is achieved.
4. In the last paragraph (lines 25–30), the writer's tone changes. By referring to sentence structure and word choice, analyse how he creates a new tone.

Answers

Answers can be found at the end of Part One, on pages 57–58.

Evaluation involves making a judgement about the success (or otherwise) of an aspect of writing.

- You could be asked to evaluate the success of a particular feature in a text – for example, the effectiveness of an image or an anecdote – in illustrating, clarifying or enlivening an article, poem or story.

- You could be asked to look at a particular section of the text and evaluate its effectiveness in clarifying the process of an argument.

- You could be asked to look at the end of an article and evaluate its success as a conclusion to the argument, the story or the 'lesson'.

Generally speaking, because great care has been taken in the choice of the passages which you are presented with, and because the writers are good at their job, the examples you are asked to evaluate are nearly always effective. What you have to do is to show what it is about the example, paragraph or article that makes it 'work' in its context. You are, however, free to make some criticism of any aspect you have to evaluate.

The following passage presents opportunities for looking at some of these possibilities.

Car trips are bad trips

Henry Ford's instrument of democratic liberation has become an oppressive tyrant, imprisoning us.

As a child, my perceptions were formed in the back of a car. The world was viewed through Triplex-toughened glass at 35mph. Notions of luxury and wellbeing were permanently influenced by the slippery leather chairs of a Humber or the curious ultraviolet light illuminating a Jaguar's walnut-veneered dashboard. Here, I was
5   psychologically secure, my regular companions a bag of crisps and a Penguin book as we motored stylishly into 'the country', wherever that used to be.

I come from the last generation to know the extraordinary institution of a recreational drive. My father, nattily dressed and moustachioed, would on certain fine days suggest an outing in the car that had no purpose other than to be an outing in the car, such was the pleasure
10   involved for all participants. There was no destination, just a circular journey: a notion as deliciously paradoxical and absurdist as a play by Samuel Beckett*. And just as historic.

The psychological aspects of driving today are altogether less comforting, as a new survey of 2000 motorists commissioned by Shell makes clear. One-third of drivers never drive for pleasure, and the rest do so only occasionally. Suffocating legislation
15   and predatory local authorities threaten to criminalise even the saintliest individual suddenly possessed by the anti-social chutzpah required to drive a car. The only rational responses to confiscatory tickets and invasive speed cameras are intense spasmodic psychomotor agitation or harrowing paranoia.

* Beckett's most famous play is *Waiting for Godot,* of which a critic said 'Nothing happens – twice'. In each act the two main characters end exactly where they started – still waiting.

20 The only rational response to traffic conditions is hysteria. Last night I met a successful businesswoman (my wife) who had been moved to hopeless tears of frustration by the barbaric tussle of driving a mere three miles in central London: a grim cast of purple-faced and cruelly determined black cab drivers, psychotic rubble-trucks, crawling buses, lost souls, and no respite from the Inferno because there is never, ever, anywhere to park. There are days, I suspect coming soon, when it will actually not be possible to complete a
25 simple car journey.

As a result, my children regard cars as unnecessary and expensive encumbrances, not the status symbol or romantic attribute they remain for me. Recent US research showed that very few people under 30 consider any automobile manufacturer to be a 'cool' brand. And those who owned cars would much prefer to keep their smartphone, if required to make a
30 competitive choice between wheeled transport and the electronic type of connectedness.

But there is poetry as well as pain here. Henry Ford created his gasoline buggy to escape from the deadening tedium of life on a Midwest farm. It is curious to consider how an instrument of democratic liberation has become an oppressive tyrant, imprisoning us.

Roads too have lost their glamour. Movies and rock music glorified some of the world's
35 great roads: Route 66, the Grande Corniche and the Pacific Coast Highway are part of our collective dreamscape. The delightful and deluded fiction of roads as romance. It is difficult, surely, to experience anything other than terrible bathos on the M25 or the East Lancashire Road.

Stephen Bayley in *The Guardian*

Task

Evaluate the effectiveness of the imagery in lines 10–11 as a conclusion to the paragraph.

Answer

The simile comparing the circular journeys they took in the car to a Samuel Beckett play is an effective conclusion because it emphasises how absurd it appears in this day and age to think that people went out for a drive to nowhere, with no purpose, just for fun.

Questions

1. Evaluate the effectiveness of the anecdote in lines 1–11 as an opening to the article.
2. Evaluate lines 26–30 as a conclusion to the contrast the writer makes between past and present driving conditions.
3. Evaluate the effectiveness of the metaphor in lines 32–33 in the context of the passage as a whole.
4. Evaluate the effectiveness of the final paragraph (lines 34–38) as a conclusion to the whole article.

Answers

Answers can be found at the end of Part One, on pages 58–59.

Conclusion

Evaluation involves you in making a judgement about the success of a piece of writing – its effectiveness.

Look carefully at what you are being asked to do. Are you being asked to deal with the passage as a whole, only part of the passage, or even just one paragraph or sentence?

Have you been asked to deal with ideas, with language, or with both?

If you are dealing with language, you should have in mind all the possibilities covered in Section 3 Analysis.

Titles, headlines and first paragraphs can be important if you are evaluating the conclusion of a passage, because an effective conclusion usually brings the whole passage into focus for you. The end often recalls or sums up in some way the initial topic or idea.

Supplementary exercise

Summer days and doing nothing

With a mixture of fear and pleasant anticipation, I stand gazing at the summer holidays, and ask myself: when did leisure become such hard work? It seems to involve more preparation than the time of the holiday itself. And when you get there there's all that 'family fun' you have to have. What's wrong with doing, well, nothing?

5   Some people believe in 'doing stuff' as a matter of principle – participating in activities, having experiences, investigating local culture and art. They worry that their children might not be used to their maximum utility. As when we are at home, schedules have to be made, lists have to be constructed, activities need to be organised.

I, on the other hand, believe that leisure is primarily about loafing, doing whatever you
10   feel like doing. The central thing about a holiday is that the clock that governs the rest of our lives is turned off briefly. You wake to write on a clean sheet. Or you can screw up the sheet, throw it away and go back to bed.

My wife is a 'doer' and I admire her drive and ambition. She has got me and the children embarking on projects that we would all have shunned if left to our own devices, chiefly
15   out of lethargy. She is a firecracker, an inexhaustible source of energy and imagination. She works hard to make sure everybody has a good time. I am actually going camping this year for the first time – an activity I have previously held as akin to a rarefied form of masochism. I may or may not enjoy it, but there is no doubt that I would not have done it without my wife to encourage me.

20   I think this schism of attitudes goes further than holiday planning, but represents two world views – the planners and the improvisers. It is the difference between the parent who perpetually worries about how their children are doing at school and makes sure that homework is done, clubs are joined, projects are completed – and the parent who is more 'light touch', believing that children have enough pressure on them as it is.

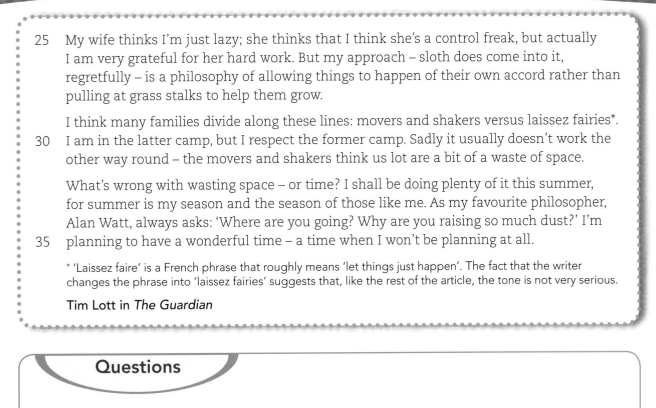

25　My wife thinks I'm just lazy; she thinks that I think she's a control freak, but actually I am very grateful for her hard work. But my approach – sloth does come into it, regretfully – is a philosophy of allowing things to happen of their own accord rather than pulling at grass stalks to help them grow.

I think many families divide along these lines: movers and shakers versus laissez fairies*.
30　I am in the latter camp, but I respect the former camp. Sadly it usually doesn't work the other way round – the movers and shakers think us lot are a bit of a waste of space.

What's wrong with wasting space – or time? I shall be doing plenty of it this summer, for summer is my season and the season of those like me. As my favourite philosopher, Alan Watt, always asks: 'Where are you going? Why are you raising so much dust?' I'm
35　planning to have a wonderful time – a time when I won't be planning at all.

* 'Laissez faire' is a French phrase that roughly means 'let things just happen'. The fact that the writer changes the phrase into 'laissez fairies' suggests that, like the rest of the article, the tone is not very serious.

Tim Lott in *The Guardian*

Questions

1. Evaluate the effectiveness of lines 20–25 in emphasising the main point the writer is making in the article as a whole.
2. Evaluate the effectiveness of the last paragraph (lines 32–35) as a conclusion to the passage. You should refer in your answer to ideas and language.

Answers

Answers can be found at the end of Part One, on page 59.

Further practice

Many of the articles used in the first three sections of this part of the book can be put to an extra use now that you have become familiar with the idea of evaluation.

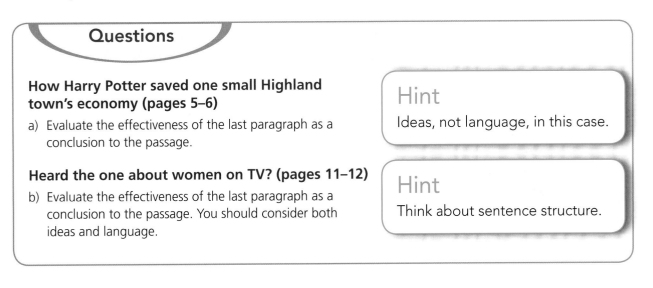

Questions

How Harry Potter saved one small Highland town's economy (pages 5–6)

a) Evaluate the effectiveness of the last paragraph as a conclusion to the passage.

Hint

Ideas, not language, in this case.

Heard the one about women on TV? (pages 11–12)

b) Evaluate the effectiveness of the last paragraph as a conclusion to the passage. You should consider both ideas and language.

Hint

Think about sentence structure.

Doctor, I feel slightly funny (pages 14–15)

c) In the last paragraph the writer says 'From an evolutionary perspective, we're just African apes on the briefest of joyrides.' Evaluate the effectiveness of this metaphor as a summary of his view in this paragraph.

d) Evaluate the effectiveness of the final paragraph as a conclusion to the passage.

A seatbelt that stops me dozing off at the wheel? Baaa humbug to that (pages 25–26)

e) Evaluate the effectiveness of the sentences 'I needed this breath … wake you up if you are.' (lines 27–30) in the structure of the passage as a whole.

Answers

Answers can be found at the end of Part One, on page 60.

SECTION 5 – SUMMARY

The first thing to be said about this section is that it is only concerned with one aspect of the skills involved in summary.

A summary in its fullest definition suggests a piece of writing that is a shorter, more concise version of the original, bringing out the important points. It is the last of these aspects – the important points – that we are going to concentrate on in this section.

You have to be able to identify the main points of the argument in both the passages you meet in the exam.

That you will have looked at the first passage in detail while you were answering the questions can be seen as helpful; but it may not be as helpful as you might think. You have to be able to stand back from the detail and focus on the main steps in the argument.

In the second passage you are given in the exam, there are no questions specifically dealing with its detail. Instead, you are instructed to read it and, 'if you wish', make notes. For 'if you wish' it is wise to substitute, in your own mind, 'you must'. How you make notes is up to you; you could underline, highlight, scribble headings, write in the margin … whatever helps you to isolate the important ideas.

You have to be able to do this because the last question in the exam paper asks you to compare the two passages in some way. This aspect is dealt with in Part Three of this book.

The focus in this chapter is on practising the skill of isolating the main point of a paragraph, or the key points of a passage, by looking at:

- topic sentences
- detail, explanation, illustration, lists, anecdote
- introductions and subheadings.

These can all help with the business of isolating important ideas, but the most helpful is definitely the topic sentence.

Topic sentences

Paragraphs are the important building blocks of any article. A good writer generally helps the reader to follow her thoughts by starting a new paragraph when the next block of the argument appears. A revision of the information in the section on explanation (Section 2, pages 7–12) would be useful here.

An aspect of good paragraph construction is that the writer signals the next step in the argument by use of a topic sentence.

The 'topic' sentence, as its name suggests, gives you an indication of the key idea in the paragraph, and the rest of the paragraph develops that topic. You should already have discussed this idea in relation to your own discursive writing.

Usually the topic sentence will be found near the beginning of the paragraph, but occasionally a writer holds the topic sentence over till the end of the paragraph – in these cases the explanation or development is building up to the main point. This is done in the following extract from an article on the definition of invasive species in the British countryside:

… even more bizarre is the presence of the barn owl on the schedule [of invasive species]. It is indisputably a native species but was put on the list to prevent uncontrolled introductions last century and so limit the spread of diseases.

The barn owl, capercaillie, chough, white-tailed eagle, all species that face being defined as non-native species, in the face of incontrovertible evidence to the contrary, are listed; the threat to them, in the face of disagreement from the bio-diversity lobby, is being ignored; the long-term consequences for the countryside are uncountable. The ultimate price is that they could all be shot.

Robert McKie in *The Observer*

The topic sentence of the second paragraph is held back to be the last statement.

Generally speaking, however, the pattern is for the topic sentence to be near the beginning of the paragraph, to set up the 'main' point. The paragraph then develops the discussion, usually to some sort of conclusion, which is often needed to complete the 'main' point.

The following simple extract is from an article about how the 'free' services provided by the world wide web are actually paid for.

We wanted the web for free – but the price is deep surveillance

'Be careful what you wish for,' runs the adage. 'You might just get it.' In the case of the internet, or at any rate the world wide web, this is exactly what happened. We wanted exciting services – email, blogging, social networking, image hosting – that were 'free'. And we got them. What we also got, but hadn't bargained for, was deep, intensive and
5   persistent surveillance of everything we do online.

We ought to have known that it would happen. There's no such thing as a free lunch, after all. Online services cost a bomb to provide: code has to be written (by programmers who have to be paid); servers have to be bought or rented, powered, housed, cooled and maintained; bandwidth has to be paid for; and so on. So there were basically only two
10   business models that could have supported our desires.

One model involved us paying for stuff. But we (or most of us, anyway) proved deeply resistant to this idea. We had the fantasy that everything online should be free, after we'd paid an ISP for a connection to the net. So paying for stuff was a non-starter.

The companies that provided the 'free' services therefore had to find another business
15   model. And in the end they found one: it was called advertising …

John Naughton in *The Observer*

Task

What is the topic covered in each of these four paragraphs?

Answer

- First paragraph: the topic is our desire to have the facilities of the internet for free, but the key idea also contains the payback for this – lack of privacy.
  So the key point of this paragraph is: the facilities of the internet come at the price of our personal privacy.
- Second paragraph: the topic is that online services have to be paid for in some way.
- Third paragraph: gives one solution – its topic – that the internet has to be paid for in monetary terms.
- Fourth paragraph: gives another solution – its topic – that the web is paid for by advertising.

Detail, explanation, illustration, lists, anecdote

As you have seen in the previous exercises, writers use any or all of these features to clarify their writing, or to expand on a point, or sometimes simply to entertain. Mostly, you have to learn to avoid all of these sections of the text when summarising the main points.

For example, the illustration about the writer's personal experience of being booked for programmes in the extract on page 12:

'I'm not a comedian but I have been told straight by TV bookers, when giving my availability to appear on something: "We already have a woman for the 19th … Could you do the 26th?"'

This is a useful little illustration, but you would not include it as a main point.

Another example of such a feature is the list below of risk limitation factors in the extract on page 26. This would have no place in a summary.

It felt old fashioned watching something potentially hazardous happen without it being surrounded by the paraphernalia of risk limitation: he didn't have to put on a mask or gloves, set a trip alarm that would go off if his skin was pierced, take a prophylactic dose of antibiotics, put the local A&E on standby, or hand me a splatter shield.

You have to be able to see where the key point lies in among all the detail. Identifying the topic sentence helps, but so does your ability to see what is necessary to explain the point and what is mere detail.

Introductions and subheadings

These can be useful in pointing you towards key concepts. For example, the subheading to the passage about Mallaig (see page 5) gives you some idea of what the key points will be.

Mallaig's days as a bustling herring port are long gone, but the town is still full of people today. Few would have guessed that its commercial salvation would be owed to a modern fairytale.

Supplementary exercises

The following passage provides an easy starter.

This short passage, written by sportswriter Hugh McIlvanney, contains only two paragraphs.

Out of love with football?

Modern football does much to sour the affections of even those of us who have been romantically involved with the game for enough years to justify throwing a diamond
5 anniversary party. It's natural to drift towards disillusionment when exposed to some of the most dispiriting trends: the increasingly tyrannical dictatorship of commercial values and attendant venality; the celebrity culture
10 that encourages too many players to show more vanity about their fame and earning power than pride in their professionalism; the reactionary stubbornness of resistance to enlisting camera evidence to help referees; or,
15 simply, the infuriating sight of penalty areas repeatedly being allowed to be engulfed by a sweaty turmoil of tag-team wrestling.

Such gloomy thoughts require an antidote and, without fail, a powerful one is
20 provided by the old, frequently disfigured game. Whatever distortions are inflicted on it, it invariably finds a way of giving lifelong devotees good reason to withstand the temptation to wonder if our commitment has been a waste of time and intensity. These days all we have to do is ask ourselves how we could possibly fall out of love with football in an era when Lionel Messi is pulling a football shirt over his head and
25 taking to the field.

Hugh McIlvanney in *The Sunday Times*

Task

What are the two key ideas in the writer's line of thought about modern football?

Answer

- Modern football has many negative values that disappoint long-term fans.
- Football always redeems itself, however, in this case with an extraordinary player.

These answers show how, in practice, you have to ignore detail.

The topic sentence in the first paragraph is the first sentence. You should not mention the long list of things that are wrong with football – these are details. The key idea is the disillusionment of the fans.

In the second paragraph, the first sentence again contains the key idea. You do, however, this time need to go further to complete the main point – that what can make football great again is a very talented player.

The following three articles become progressively more difficult, and the tasks associated with them become more complicated. The aim is to isolate the key ideas. Sometimes you will be given the number of key ideas to guide you; at other times you are left to your own devices. Generally, in the length of passages used, you are probably looking for no more than three or four key areas.

Look out for repetition of the same idea in different paragraphs, with different examples. In these cases you should mention the key idea only once.

Proof at last: being fat is not our fault

The fatter we become, the less willing we are to change.

A new book attempts to explain that we are not entirely to blame for our ever-expanding global girth. Equally culpable is the hand that literally feeds us. The book by David A. Kessler is a long-overdue tome detailing the myriad ways in which the food industry conspires to exploit us. It designs food to contain as much sugar, fat and salt as possible,

5 to hit what's known inside the industry as 'the three points of the compass'. The use of these specific components, which give food its most addictive 'moreish' qualities, not only manipulates our psychology (as ever) but uses science to manipulate our very biology, to feed the insatiable (financial) greed of the food industry.

After millennia of stable human weight, the past 20 years has seen an explosion in

10 average weights following an explosion of what scientists call 'palatable' food. These are foods that are not only lip-smackin', they actively stimulate appetite by stimulating neurons, which trigger the brain's reward system and release the dopamine bullseye, kick-starting a vicious cycle. This is achieved by loading sugar, fat and salt into core ingredients such as meat, veg, potatoes and bread. The not-so-curiously addictive

15 Frappuccino® hosts 16 spoonfuls of sugar. Basic foods are subject to the irresistible 'layering' gambit (smothered in cheese, cream or sauce – or all three).

Bombarded every day by 'highly salient stimuli' that skew our pleasure and reward systems, our natural chewing instincts have halved over 20 years (foods are created with speedy and ultimately unsatisfying 'mouth-melt' properties). We are also addicted to

20 carbonation processes that stimulate the trigeminal nerve, which then seeks out further stimulation – and on it goes in a world of meticulously engineered food combinations that ensure conditioned hyper-eating. And before you know it you're a 60-stone human waterbed on a reinforced surgical hospital trolley the width of the average hovercraft.

We can though, according to Kessler, fight back – through enforced labelling,

25 implementing portion control and aggressively battling our increasingly ruinous urges. And one day, he predicts, we'll become 'deconditioned' and view our idiotic food choices as we do tobacco today, as a deadly, addictive product. But, as Kessler points out: 'We can live without tobacco. Food is much harder.'

Sylvia Patterson in *The Herald*

Question

1. What are the three key ideas in this passage?

Answer

The answer can be found at the end of Part One, on page 60.

BBC is shutting out young Britain

The planned 'migration' of BBC3 to the internet and the corporation's iPlayer in the autumn of 2015 means that 'Youth', that segment of the BBC's audience with the least political power and the fewest public voices, will become an afterthought.

5 The strange late-night pleasures of the imported *Family Guy* aside, I don't watch BBC3. Equally, I question its credentials as the home of youthful innovation when I note a slew of *Doctor Who* and *Top Gear* reruns on an evening-only channel. But BBC3 isn't aimed at me. For me, and for the rest of the white, middle-aged licence-fee payers who dominate arguments over the corporation's output, there are plenty of alternatives.

Some would say the corporation's rapid expansion at the start of the century now looks 10 like hubris. The attempt to provide a dedicated service to all ages and all interests in a multi-channel world might have been passed off as a modern version of the old BBC mission to educate, inform and entertain; but it appears to have been misjudged.

You could ask how the hard financial choices are made – and why. BBC3 has 13 million viewers a week. In August last year, Radio 4 hit a 'record-breaking' weekly score of 15 10.97 million. Which group has more rights? Or rather, which group is better placed to influence those who run the BBC? To whom would politicians listen?

The answer is obvious. If you believe that the *Today* programme is a bit more important to society than *Snog Marry Avoid?*, you are liable to think the obvious answer is the right answer. But the BBC3 viewer base embraces close to a million of the young unemployed – 20 less likely to be white and middle class than the Radio 4 fan base; more likely to be excluded from the political process. They are no match for the grey power of pensioners.

For my taste, most of the things on BBC3 are rubbish. To be accurate, though, most of the things on most channels are rubbish. But I can take consolation in the fact that the BBC will go on trying to cater to my interests and tastes for a long time to come, just as it will 25 go on serving up *EastEnders* and witless talent shows to those numerous enough not to be seen as a minority.

For whom *does* the BBC exist? The minority – young Britain – just got pushed unceremoniously to the back of the queue.

Ian Bell in *The Sunday Herald*

Questions

1. Identify the topic of each paragraph.
2. From these identify the really key ideas.

Answers

Answers can be found at the end of Part One, on page 61.

The madness of crowds

John Donne's observation that people are not isolated entities – 'No man is an island' – is not quite true, because there are indeed solitaries, anchorites and society-shunning misanthropes among us; but it is nearly so, because it captures the fact that, as essentially social animals, we need our connections with others, our friendships and our
5   exchanges of affection and dependency.

This is what explains the phenomenon of taking sides. You might be watching a sporting event in which you have no particular interest regarding who wins, and yet you soon find yourself preferring one side to the other. It is hard to stay aloof in any division of opinion, any quarrel or conflict. Sometimes one can think, 'A plague on both your houses,' but
10 that is a relatively rare state of disinterest. We like to belong, even vicariously.

This group thinking was no doubt of evolutionary advantage to our earliest forebears, given that clubbing together against a tiger or a gang of marauding strangers has obvious survival value. In more recent times, the natural inclination to get caught up in group feeling has had less constructive outcomes. The madness of crowds, their manipulability
15 by demagogues, the collective blood-lust of lynch-mobs, are frightening examples of how something monstrous still lurks below the individual level of consciousness, making people do as one of a mob what one would never dream of doing on one's own.

Some would hotly deny that supporting a football club or the national team has anything to do with the hysteria of a mass rally at Nuremberg. The good-natured singing in the
20 stands, the sense of affinity with thousands of like-minded folk wearing the same-coloured scarves, is of course a thing to be celebrated: it is a paradigm of the harmony of togetherness, at least on one side of the ground. The point is that it is not just in very different circumstances, in bad places and times, that the same community of sentiment can go horribly wrong on those self-same stands.

25 Yet John F. Kennedy famously said that hell's hottest depths are kept for those who stay neutral and don't take sides when the moral stakes are high. He is surely right; the idea that not taking sides against the perpetrators of evil is to be complicit in their evil.

On the other hand – why, someone once asked, were we given two hands if we weren't to make use of the fact? – there are plenty of cases where impartiality, objectivity,
30 disinterestedness are key to what makes civilisation civilised. The administration of justice; scientific exploration; education; adjudication of competing interests in the daily life of commerce and trade; fairness in the allocation of resources and social goods – in all these cases bias distorts and causes harm. The very meaning of co-operation is that all parties are on the same side, rather than splitting into opposed sides.

35 But here are some sides it is always worth being on: the side of generosity and tolerance, of the bullied against the bullies, of peace against war – these are the sides one should always take, even if it costs.

It goes without saying that in other aspects of life, the fine judgement we all must be capable of making is: when to take sides and when not. That is what it is to be wise.

A. C. Grayling in *Prospect Magazine*

Questions

The writer of the passage is presenting two views on 'taking sides'.

1. Make a list of the positive points made about taking sides.
2. Make a list of the negative points made about taking sides.
3. Make a note of any key points in the article that are not included in these two lists.

Answers

Answers can be found at the end of Part One, on page 61.

Conclusion

Paragraph structure can help to identify key ideas.

Cut out unnecessary details, examples, lists, and so on.

Opening statements and subheadings can point towards a key idea.

There may be some points that are quite similar, where the ideas overlap, so you should try to generalise, to blend them into one idea.

List of terms used

Topic sentence, key idea, generalisation.

ANSWERS TO QUESTIONS IN PART ONE

Section 1 – Identification

Robot cars – made by Google

1. • Fight wars.
   • Undertake vastly expensive programmes on behalf of the state.

> ## Commentary
>
> Look for the word 'state' or 'states' in the paragraph. These are the signposts that alert you to the two separate points made about the state's potential.
>
> But notice that you have to take the idea and put it in your own words.
>
> The phrase given in the answer – 'undertake vastly expensive programmes on behalf of the state' is recasting the idea of 'A state put a man on the Moon, another massive costly enterprise'.

2. • The ability to pinpoint position.
   • Advanced computer technology.

3. • The regulations governing driverless traffic on the roads.
   • The wish to retain conventional, human-driven cars.
   • Managing the move from one system to another.

> ## Commentary
>
> You are expected to generalise each of the phrases used in the passage – for example 'the wish to retain conventional cars' combines or generalises the three sets of people – those who don't want driverless cars, those who can't afford driverless cars and those who enjoy driving.

4. • The road system.
   • The insurance industry.
   • The legal system.

> ## Commentary
>
> In some places the answers can simply use the words in the passage: 'the insurance industry'/'the legal system'. In these cases there is no sensible 'translation' available. The words are not difficult.

How Harry Potter saved one small Highland town's economy

1. • Railway reached Mallaig in 1901.
   • One of the last railways built.
   • Used concrete for viaducts.
   • Passed through spectacular and uninhabited scenery.
   • Needed a lot of government money to build.
   • Never carried enough people or freight.
   • Never a viable enterprise.
   • Faced with closure in the 1960s.
   • Saved by hobbyists and Harry Potter fans.

> **Commentary**
>
> In each of these cases, after the first mention of the railway there is a mention of 'it' or 'its', showing that the fact that follows is about the railway.

2. • Railway reached Mallaig in 1901.
   • Needed a lot of government money to build.
   • Never economically viable.
   • Faced with closure in the 1960s.
   • Saved by hobbyists and Harry Potter fans.

> **Commentary**
>
> The ability to distinguish important facts from a number of less important ones is a skill that you will need in Section 4 Evaluation and Section 5 Summary. In this answer, it is possible that the first item in this list is the least important.

3. • Many locomotives were preserved by devotees.
   • Many branch lines were saved.

4. • An actual historical figure (Bonnie Prince Charlie) was there.
   • He actually raised his flag to rally supporters there.
   • There is a massive 60ft memorial that provides evidence that it's all true.

> **Commentary**
>
> The helpful word here is 'real' or 'reality'. The writer uses it three times to emphasise the historical actuality in the face of the fictional myth.

Section 2 – Explanation

Sometimes it is right to wipe out a species

1. He sees such an extinction as (undoubtedly) a great positive for mankind.

> ### Commentary
> All you have to do here is explain what 'an unambiguously good thing' means. The context helps you, because 'a good thing' tells you that he views it positively; 'unambiguously' – even if you don't know what it means – must obviously strengthen that idea; and 'Be in no doubt' gives you the idea that unambiguously means that there is no possible room for doubt of any kind. The context has helped you to your answer.

2. His use of mosquitoes as an example shows that an ecosystem would only be slightly affected by the elimination of one species out of 2500; that if one species were got rid of others would take its place.

3. The extra genes in the male mean that its offspring cannot reproduce, so fewer will be born. This means that available females will gradually only have the genetically modified males to breed with, which will result in even more infertile mosquitoes. Eventually all the mosquitoes in a given area will be infertile and so the species will have been eliminated.

> ### Commentary
> Signposts such as 'the rarer', 'the better', 'so', 'more effective, not less', help you to see your way through this paragraph.

4. It might upset the balance of nature as it now stands, and we might not worry about extinction on the grounds that we could always reverse it. But most importantly it is going beyond the bounds of what humans should be doing to the world – too much like playing God.

> ### Commentary
> The argument goes from 'It might …' to 'or make us …' to 'Worse …', so there is evidently a climactic argument going on, the last part being the most important.

Heard the one about women on TV?

1. Because they are not booked for TV, and thus don't earn enough money to afford to go on tour and practise their art and become more famous.

2. If they don't earn money from TV, they can't afford to go on tour – or, they have to earn money in some other way by having a job, which then also prevents them from having the free time to go on tour. And if they can't move outside their own area, they can't become better known and thus get a chance to be on TV – so they can't earn the money to go on tour, which lands them back exactly where they started.

> ### Commentary
> The words that will help you through this circular argument are ones such as 'If … either … nor … if they can't … they won't … so they won't …'

3. If a show falls flat the producers will assume the failure was because the comic was a woman, rather than that she just had an off night. And audience laughter is sometimes not the best measure of success, as an audience may feel a bit on edge because the comic is a woman and they don't feel comfortable about that, or because the woman may be making jokes at the expense of men, which is not the 'normal' expected outcome of jokes.

Commentary

This is quite a large section of text to deal with, but sentence structure will help here, as it did in the previous section on identification.

- In lines 21–24, there is a contrast between 'an obscure male comic' and 'a woman … however …'
- In lines 28, 'It's not just … crowds are too', is followed by two reasons for the crowd's behaviour – that they are 'nervous' on behalf of the woman and feel 'irritated' at a woman demonstrating superiority.

4. The instruction to include 'at least one woman', aimed at increasing female representation, will be narrowly interpreted as only one per show, no matter how many men there are, so it will not achieve the goal of equal participation.

Commentary

Although this is a very simple question, you can see how the writer's anecdote about her own experience of being booked for shows makes the situation clearer.

5. The writer thinks it important because television in some sense plays a big part in forming impressions of society in the viewers' minds. And if women are unrepresented, or are in an incorrect ratio to men, then society's debate is not functioning properly.

Section 3 – Analysis

Doctor, I feel slightly funny

1. - 'pin it on' suggests that the politicians are trying to blame people for overusing the NHS, in the same way that you would pin a crime on someone.
   - 'lard-buckets' suggests that people eat too much greasy food and so become repositories of fatty grease – quite a revolting thought – needing care from the NHS.
   - 'frittered' gives the impression of a carelessness with resources – just letting them fall away in little useless bits – the money for the NHS is not being used constructively.

Commentary

The use of 'suggests' or 'gives the impression of' allows you to move into the connotations of the word, rather than its simple meaning. You do not have to mention what the denotation of the word is. That is self-evident. The important element is connotation.

2. - 'scraped off the pavement' gives the impression of somebody having had a really serious accident (possibly a road accident) that has resulted in blood and guts on the pavement and therefore created an opportunity for the NHS to do what it was really set up to do.

- 'life's little problems' suggests that trivial things are regarded as medical emergencies. The tone of the phrase is mocking (see page 27 on Tone) and the alliteration of the insubstantial sound 'l' adds to the light and unimportant feeling.

3. • 'defusing' suggests that the anxiety people feel about their health is dangerous and needs to be snuffed out before it explodes, causing real harm.
   - 'worried-well' is a phrase that uses juxtaposition – that is, the putting together of two conflicting words – to draw your attention to the pairing. In this case the two words are apparent contradictions – if you are well you should not be worried. It gives the impression of people making things up in order to call on medical help.
   - 'doomed (pursuit)' suggests that they will never be able to find the solution; the pursuit is a dead end.
   - 'pathologically (anxious)' suggests that the anxiety is a disease in itself – something exaggerated and out of proportion.

Commentary

Juxtaposition is putting together two words in such a way that they cause the reader to think again and to look more closely. When they are contradictory, as here, the technical term is 'oxymoron'. (You don't have to use the term, as long as you can explain the effect.)

4. • 'Social phobia' sounds like a medical condition, whereas 'shyness' is just a description of a fairly common human trait. The term 'social phobia' is used by drug companies because they feel that by giving it a scientific name, they can sell a scientific cure.

5. • The words the writer chooses to describe the pills suggest that he doesn't think very much of their clinical effects.
   - 'dubious' suggests that there is no proof they have a good effect – he really doubts it.
   - 'exotic' suggests that people believe that these things must be effective because they have strange and foreign-sounding names.
   - 'tinctures, linctuses, powders, pearls and salts': each of these suggests an old-fashioned remedy, a kind of traditional or folkloric or alternative solution to problems – probably unproven by any real science – more like a sort of witchcraft.

Commentary

In the case of 'tinctures, linctuses, powders, pearls and salts' you would probably choose just one to comment on, because the same comment can really apply to all of the items.

'Sounds of the day'

1. • 'clatter' suggests a hard sound, jangling and not gentle.
   - 'creaked' suggests the high-pitched sound of the lapwing – but not pleasant-sounding birdsong.
   - 'snuffling puff' suggests a wet breathy sound caused by the waves on the rock.
   - 'black drums rolled' – the sound of water falling from a height constantly beating on the rock below and creating an ominous sound.

Commentary

These words have to be taken in the context of the whole poem, so you know that you are not dealing with pleasant, warm, gentle sounds.

2. • 'scraped' is a harsh sound, reminiscent of sounds that set your teeth on edge, which corresponds with the poet's/persona's feelings of sadness and desolation.

3. • The repetition of 'was' constantly reminds the poet (and the reader) of the absolute separation of those times that are now past, from the sad present.

4. • 'plunge' suggests the suddenness of the action and a sort of desperation in the action.
   • 'freezing' gives an impression of the numbing effect of cold water, the shock of the change.
   • 'bangle of ice' suggests a constriction, an unpleasant, hostile feeling.
   • 'whole' suggests that the effects of the cold spread unstoppably.
   • 'numb' suggests that as the hand becomes incapable of bearing any more pain and so feeling shuts down, so the mental hurt freezes his emotions.

   These cold and hard words are effective in drawing attention to the devastating effects of the end of the relationship.

Commentary

It is sometimes difficult to make an absolute distinction between word choice and imagery. In the following section, there is a detailed discussion of imagery (pages 18–19). In all cases, however, the connotations of the words are important. 'A bangle of ice' is actually a metaphor, which has its own effectiveness, but equally the word 'bangle', a pleasurable ornament to the wearer, is here almost like a constricting band, and is effective as word choice.

At the Loch of the Green Corrie

1. • 'the scree curtain' is a metaphor that suggests the idea of a huge curtain with folds in the fabric that represents the uneven surface of the cliff of stones wrapping round the lochan. This is effective in giving the impression of the hidden and enclosed space the lochan occupies.
   • 'as reclining on a high balcony' is a simile giving the impression that the lochan is rather lazily perched high above the space below the hill – perfectly at ease.
   • 'the water … impatiently swatted away the light' is a metaphor (in this case a personification) because the water is being given the human characteristic of being able to use a hand to dissipate light on its surface. Here it gives the impression that the water is in control of what the fisherman sees in or on it.
   • 'green ropes' is a metaphor that lets us see the thickness and capacity of the water weed, perhaps to capture and hold as ropes can.

2. a) 'fresh cast snags the ruffled water', and b) 'a clockwork fisherman running down'.
   a) The line he casts tears at the water, causing it to ruffle in the same way that a rough edge can cause a thread to pull a piece of material out of shape making its surface uneven, giving a detail of the way he sees the water's surface changing.
   b) The impression this metaphor gives is of the fisherman becoming tired after a long time fishing, and as if he had been wound up like a clockwork toy at the beginning of the day. The spring has now wound down and his movements will become slower and slower until eventually he stops, incapable of any further movement.

   Probably the clockwork fisherman is the more effective metaphor, as it concerns an important actor in the scene, and paints a vivid picture of tiredness.

Commentary

What you are doing when you state a preference is actually making an evaluation – which we will discuss in Section 4. You are at liberty to choose either of these images; there is no one correct answer here.

3. • 'bleak screescape' – it is possible to discuss this as word choice in the sense that the blend of bleak, scree and scape suggests an inhospitable landscape. 'screescape' could be treated metaphorically in that it blends the idea of a landscape, which could be pleasant, with a vast area of scree slope, which gives a harsh and barren impression.
   • 'the travelling slash of ripples' suggests the sharp movements of the water caused by the breeze pushing currents across the surface (word choice). Metaphorically, part of the water could be seen as setting out to cut its way, as if it were a knife, through the surface of the lochan.
   • 'becomes riddled with grey' suggests that many small areas of grey caused by the fading of the light are permeating the surface, darkening the surface of the water. Metaphorically, the little patches of darkness that descend on the water are like the small sprinklings of ash or earth falling from the mesh of a riddle, giving an impression of the progressive darkening of the surface of the water.

Commentary

The analysis of these phrases shows how word choice and metaphor often blend into each other. The actual identification of a phrase is not as important as your ability to express the effect that the phrase gives, either literally, figuratively or both.

4. • 'growling burn' – an example of personification suggests that the burn itself is annoyed or angry with the landscape, or with the weather or the fisherman, contributing to the cold, uncomfortable atmosphere.
   • 'a hunchback' – a metaphor describing the fisherman as if he were permanently disabled and unable to move properly because of the hump on his back, when in fact his inability to move properly is as a result of carrying a backpack – it gives the impression that he is too burdened and heavy to move, contributing to the atmosphere of discomfort.

The Telegram

1. The similes 'like … a fat domestic bird' and 'more like a buzzard' give a very quick and graphic distinction between the two women, as a domestic bird is usually seen as something homely and rounded, completely harmless, or maybe over-protected and lazy – while a buzzard suggests a bird of prey, more angular and dangerous, or maybe just having to work harder to survive.

2. The imagery of the plague is effective, as the war is being seen as a disease which kills in large numbers, regardless of fairness, in the same way that an infectious disease infects some by chance, but not others.

3. The comparison of the telegram to a 'strange missile' is effective, in that it emphasises the deadly nature of the news in the telegram, which can kill from a distance, and saying it 'picked a door' continues the idea of the random nature of the deaths. The association of 'weapon' leaving desolation in its wake describes accurately the effect of the telegram.

Bilingualism is good for you. But monoglots needn't despair

1. The dash introduces a definition of 'the Sapir-Whorf hypothesis'.

Commentary

A colon could have been used here instead of a dash, but the tone of the explanation is quite light and informal ('the deliciously sci-fi name'), so the slightly less formal introduction of an explanation is acceptable (and perhaps even preferable) in this context.

2. This is another use of the declarative sentence, again stressing his delight at the concept of bilingualism.

The second function is as a link moving from the advantage of bilingualism that ends the previous paragraph into the idea that bilingual children are luckier than he was – which is the subject of the next paragraph.

3. The parallelism of this sentence emphasises the children's ignorance of the language – 'magical incantations' balances with 'abracadabra'. Both are examples of meaningless use of language.

4. The colon (line 23) in this sentence prepares us for an explanation of or, in this case, examples of the distortion. There is an explanation of each of the two distortions separated by a semi-colon. This helps the reader to recognise where one explanation finishes and the other begins. Each explanation gives the literal meaning of the phrase in inverted commas and then gives a further, clearer meaning after a dash. This clearer meaning is also marked out by its being put in inverted commas.

Commentary

The use of italics to represent the words in Farsi could also have been mentioned, although it is a typographical device rather than a punctuation feature.

5. The effort he made initially is shown by his use of a list of items after the colon in line 36. The number of things he piled up to help him shows that he was trying, although the final item in the list – a large stock of chocolate – is perhaps a bit of an anti-climax. It shows that ultimately he was perhaps less serious than he should have been.

The dash in line 37 introduces a list of reasons that account for his failure to learn at that age. Again the list of items climaxes with a rather immature reaction to self-discipline – he needed a threat to keep him at it.

Commentary

In dealing with sentence structure, especially where you are dealing with punctuation, it is good practice to identify the dash, or the list, by a line reference. In this paragraph there are two lists, and a slightly different comment is required for each, so it is necessary to identify which list you are talking about.

6. The last sentence uses a colon to introduce a repetition of the ideas that were dealt with in the opening paragraphs about bilingualism. His use of parenthesis '– or, better still, to pass on –' aimed at parents rather than just the children, widens out his plea. The last clause, an imperative clause, is a command to his readers. It brings the article to a climax, which emphasises the positive tone of the whole article.

A seatbelt that stops me dozing off at the wheel? Baaa humbug to that

1. The structure of the first sentence is effective as the reader is waiting for the explanation following the colon of what the 'old fashioned experience' was – and the explanation seems to be rather ordinary, an anti-climax.

The second sentence ends with a climax: 'pizzas … reds of a festering wound', and gives a vivid and exaggerated description of food that the writer hopes will capture the reader's attention.

Commentary

It becomes obvious that this article is dealing with quite a serious subject, but is introducing the ideas with rather a jokey tone that allows the writer to use such devices as exaggeration and sarcasm. This will be dealt with in the next section on Tone.

2. This sentence acts as a link. '[And] It wasn't just … old fashioned way' from 'old fashioned' in paragraph 1. It shows that the writer is going on to describe more 'old fashioned' aspects of his experience.

> ### Commentary
> It is helpful to your understanding of the argument of a passage to be able to recognise these 'links' between paragraphs – even though you may not be asked a specific question about them.

3. Only two examples are given of cheating 'slightly' (examples of what is 'non-meat' in the shop), whereas cheating 'massively' is expanded by giving an extremely long list showing the number and variety of possible massive cheats – 'out-of-town location … probably actual houses'. The list is made more effective by the climactic last item 'actual houses', which is obviously an exaggeration put in for effect.

> ### Commentary
> It is good practice to identify which list you are talking about – especially in an article like this where there are several examples.

4. 'And' at the beginning of the sentence, where its use is unconventional, makes the reader pay more attention to the sentence; the repetition of 'fingers' keeps our attention fixed on the vulnerability of the butcher's unprotected hands.

> ### Commentary
> It is always worthwhile looking out for uses of language that are not 'normal' or conventional – as here, beginning the sentence with 'And'. Normally there would not have been a new sentence – the 'and' clause would just have been joined on to the previous statement.
>
> Sometimes the word order is unexpected – as in 'And his fingers, let's not forget, are basically …' The more normal word order would be 'And let's not forget his fingers are basically …' The writer has used this change in word order so that we focus on 'his fingers' and what might happen to them.

5. The modern obsession with risk is continued by the writer noticing that a dangerous activity is being carried out without modern safety procedures. This is given emphasis by his illustration, after the colon, of all the sorts of different things that the modern world seems to judge necessary in a risky situation. Again the writer ends the list with a climax 'or hand me a splatter shield', which would suggest that he might need to be protected from being sprayed by the butcher's blood if the butcher gets it wrong.

The simplicity of the short last sentence of the paragraph – 'He just knew what he was doing.' – contrasts with the elaborate rituals of risk management detailed in the previous sentence. It tends to show the writer's bias in favour of the simpler, more old fashioned solution.

> ### Commentary
> Both parts of the answer keep the question in mind – 'How is the idea of the modern obsession with risk emphasised'; the analysis is linked to the original question. Notice again that the answer identifies which short sentence is being analysed.

6. The first example is the paragraph's opening sentence, 'I know that … at all'. The punctuation helps by allowing a contrast to be made between the parenthesis in the first part of the sentence, 'at first glance', and the parenthesis in the second part of the sentence, 'on consideration'. The contrast is again emphasised by the use of the semi-colon. This acts as a pivot on which the sentence turns, moving the idea from being 'incontrovertibly good' to 'a bad idea'. The sentence thus acts as an introduction to the rest of the article about the disadvantages of Harken.

    A second example of punctuation is the writer's use of parenthesis in lines 38–40. The two dashes serve to include examples of what can go wrong with newly 'improved' car technology. This allows the writer to exercise his sarcasm, showing how bad ideas can spring from supposed improvements.

Commentary

The first of these examples can be described as a 'balanced sentence' – there are two halves, each of which deals with aspects of the same subject.

It could also be described as a 'parallel sentence' – at first glance good; on consideration bad.

Because there is an opposition between the two parts of the sentence, it could be described as an antithesis or an antithetical sentence.

It actually doesn't matter too much which term is used, so long as the answer shows that the construction being in two 'halves' makes the ideas clearer.

Out of office reply: I'm on hols but please keep me up to speed

1. The writer is only pretending to be shocked. The tone is exaggerated: 'affliction' suggests we are suffering from a disease. He is making too much of it – rather as he did in the opening sentences.

2. The factual point is that the French (or one of the big French unions) is trying to draw a line between work hours and leisure hours, so that workers' personal time is not eaten into. The stereotyping in the phrase 'cheese-eating, work-shy surrender monkeys' is referring, in a less-than-serious way, to the shorter working hours, and is trivialising the idea by adding the stereotypical image of the French liking for cheese.

3. The factual point is that a German firm has issued orders about the deletion of emails for employees who are on holiday, suggesting a rigorous approach – but he undercuts it with the stereotype of the German on holiday monopolising the best sun loungers, again less than seriously.

4. An obsession with health and safety and football are the two aspects of life in the UK that he chooses to represent British concerns – again poking fun at national stereotypes.

5. The simile 'as if preparing for a mission to the dark side of the Moon' exaggerates the deprivation of going without your phone for a week by comparing it with the hardships of space travel – a laughable comparison.

    (It would also be possible to discuss 'digital detox' and 'diet du jour', both of which imply that the consumption of communications is as important as that of what actually keeps one alive – food and drink.)

6. The writer has deliberately exaggerated the power of the app – an electric shock is a bit severe as a punishment, not to mention dangerous. His 'apology' in parenthesis gives the impression of 'pretend' truthfulness – mocking/attacking the overuse of phones, and so on.

7. 'Lost a whole afternoon to it.' This short sentence sums up the problems of the internet. The fact that the writer himself has become hooked and wasted his time shows that he is not immune, and adds to the idea that he is not really attacking us, more gently mocking human behaviour – including his own.

8. The kind of commanding tone used in these final sentences recalls the mock complaining tone of the opening. The middle sentence admits that probably nobody has listened to him, as they have all been fully occupied with their phones, and so on. The last, single-word sentence is a recognition that nothing will change. The tone could be described as one of resignation.

Commonwealth Games

1. • For a television critic to be so casual about when and what he is attempting to comment on shows that he is not launching into a normal criticism of a show. The three dots (aposiopesis is the technical name for this use of three dots; ellipsis is different – check it out) suggest a carelessness about the show, as if it wasn't worthwhile taking it seriously. His use of 'anyway' suggests that he really couldn't care less when it was – it's not important. And his vagueness about the actual title of the show is sort of insulting, as if he is above such things.

2. • Calling the Commonwealth a 'club' suggests something friendly and supportive, which is in direct contrast with the abusive treatment described in the next list. It makes the existence of such an organisation almost unbelievable, thus contributing to the tone of mock disbelief.
   • The list of actions – 'invaded, imprisoned … patronised by the limeys' – suggests that our treatment of the countries Britain 'annexed' was excessively bad, both in the number and violence of the actions. Comment could be made on word choice relating to any of the items in the list – 'exploited' and 'patronised' would probably be the easiest to use.
   • 'get together … to play games' is deliberately childish in tone and contrasts with the Games' far more serious origins in the colonisation of these countries.
   • The tone of 'Really' is that of someone who finds it very difficult to accept the previous statement.
   • The contrast between 'honeymoon destinations' and 'Glasgow', which does not usually top the list for a romantic holiday, makes the whole idea of holding the Games in Glasgow seem incongruous.
   • 'It's August, it's Scotland, of course it rained.' is a declarative sentence – nobody is going to dispute the statement, making Glasgow sound like an even more unlikely place for the Games to be held.

> ## Commentary
> You would never be asked to provide so many examples in an exam question; but here, because we are practising the skill of recognising and commenting on tone, you have been asked to do more.
>
> 'Incongruous' is a useful word when commenting on tone. Incongruity is the result often of a mismatch that is laughable, caused (as it is here) by the juxtaposition of two conflicting ideas.

3. • The lack of resources and size of the smaller of the 71 nations is exaggerated by the writer's description of their being 'taken over by a wooden gunboat and 20 Highlanders with dysentery' – where 'wooden' suggests that they didn't need any high-tech weaponry, and 20 sick soldiers suggests that they didn't need an army – that is, that the British had an unfair advantage.
   • 'to beat them at games for which the British write the rules' suggests that the British are still in charge, and that they set up unfair circumstances in which they can win.
   • The word choice of 'jingoism' and 'jockism' are derogatory terms for nationalism, and 'teeniest bit embarrassing' is using an exaggeratedly 'small' criticism to point out how really embarrassing it is.

> ## Commentary
> You have been asked to find two examples, but it is worthwhile looking at all of the answers given here to get more idea of the range of answers possible in a 'tone' question.

- The contrast between 'small gamely developing' and 'the fifth biggest economy in the world' shows the unfair advantage that the home nations have.
- 'on our knees in gratitude' is creating a deliberately demeaning picture to suggest that our attitude should not be one of superiority, because, in real terms, we have nothing to be superior about.
- The imagery in the last sentence of the paragraph – 'We look like the fat … his garden.' – is effective as it makes the home nations seem like bullies who have to have it all their own way, rather than making sure that the 'guests' feel valued while on their property.

4.
- The tone changes from being openly, if mockingly, critical of the Games to being superficially nice about the idea. The writer belittles their importance and drama, however, so that he is still being critical but using irony instead of mockery.
- The use of the colon in line 26 introduces a deflating description of the Games – 'gently exciting' does not suggest any great drama or struggle.
- The similar structure of the next two sentences adds to the cosy, undemanding and unexciting nature of the Games. For example, the advantage is that it's still on good old terrestrial TV, and it doesn't have the disadvantage of being unsportsmanlike or violent. Such comparisons tend to belittle the importance and passion of the Games.
- The last sentence also demeans the Games, in that the final comment is not on winners and losers, but on the comfortable companionship of a familiar, dependable (and possibly boring) commentator.
- For word choice there are a number of possible examples. The easiest to comment on are probably 'gently exciting' and 'that nice …'.

Commentary

This is quite a difficult question to answer as the tone changes dramatically in the last paragraph, where the writer appears to be complimentary about the Games but is, in fact, still maintaining the criticism by ironically, or even sarcastically, praising them.

Section 4 – Evaluation

Car trips are bad trips

1. The anecdote is effective as an introduction to the article because the writer is mainly being critical of the present horrible driving conditions. So the gentle, pleasurable portrait of what driving used to be like makes the modern way seem even more awful by contrast.

2. This paragraph sums up the contrast the writer has been making throughout – by referring to his children's experience as opposed to his own. They have no pleasurable memories of motoring and regard it as a waste of time and money. The contrast is made even more obvious when he compares the two forms of 'connectedness'; the physical ability of a car to connect people and places is less important now that smartphones and the internet make for increased connection and communication of another kind.

3. 'an instrument of democratic liberation' refers to the car, and the freedom it gave in the early days, but 'an oppressive tyrant, imprisoning us' makes it seem as if the car has now become a domineering box that confines us forcibly in unpleasant conditions. The political contrast between a democracy and a tyranny is an effective metaphor to illustrate the complete change that has happened to motoring.

4. The last paragraph makes an effective conclusion for the writer's argument because it reminds us of where the passage started – with the descriptions of the pleasure of motoring in the old days. This is done by giving us a romantic description of the legendary long-distance routes that pioneer motorists travelled, with romantic names like the Grande Corniche. But then he contrasts these ideas with the mundane and horrible conditions that exist now, citing boring roads with boring names.

Commentary

In this sort of question, you can be asked to consider the effectiveness of the ideas, or of the ideas **and** the language. In the answer above, the main thrust is on ideas, but if the question had asked you 'to consider ideas **and** language' you could have dealt with: such words as 'collective dreamscape', 'roads as romance'; the effect of the list of exotic names; the use of contrast (M25 and the Grande Corniche); or any other feature you noticed. Remember that use of language covers any of the features discussed in Section 3 Analysis.

Note on evaluation

You could say that the final paragraph is not really a very effective conclusion, as it introduces a new set of ideas and doesn't do very much with them.

And you could comment on such words as 'glorified', 'dreamscape' or 'deluded', which suggest that the writer has an unrealistic, false memory of motoring in the past that undermines the contrast he is trying to make between then and now. In general, however, it is safe to assume that your evaluation is likely to be positive.

Summer days and doing nothing

1. This paragraph gives very neatly the central idea of the article – that there is a distinct division into two sorts of people. It generalises from the writer's own particular circumstances, thus making the article generally relevant, before going on to illustrate further from his own experience. This paragraph is effective as a pivoting point in the article.

2. The concluding paragraph is effective in revealing his solution – not to plan. This recalls the opening of the article, which asked the question about why one should plan – and despite the efforts of his wife (and all 'doers') he still retains his own preferences.

The tone of the conclusion is light-hearted – as suits what he is going to do. He picks up on the 'waste of space' idea from the previous paragraph and turns it into a justification for his own behaviour. The repetition of 'summer' recalls the reference to 'summer holidays' in the first paragraph.

Finally, he plays on the word 'planning' to emphasise that what he is doing is actually the reverse.

Commentary

It is good practice to refer to the passage throughout (but especially its opening), showing how the last paragraph recalls, sums up or reverses the initial idea.

Further practice

How Harry Potter saved one small Highland town's economy

a) This paragraph is effective as a conclusion because it puts in summary form the two things that have been the subject of the article – steam engines and Harry Potter films – linking them to the economic recovery of Mallaig. It also takes us back to the introduction to the article – the economy of Mallaig.

Heard the one about women on TV?

b) This paragraph is effective as a conclusion to the article because the writer uses it to draw important general conclusions from the previous material about women's under-representation in comedy. It's not just about the number of female comics on TV – it's about the much wider problem of how society's views can be distorted by the balance of sexes represented on TV.

Sentence structure is also effective – the two questions at the beginning of the paragraph are designed to start people thinking. The declarative sentence 'And yet I do … importance' puts the writer's viewpoint strongly. The sentence beginning 'Whether' followed by a list of TV genres, then 'if' followed by a list of 'classes' of people, leads up to the important point the reader has been waiting for – 'that conversation is weakened and our opinions misshapen'. The short final sentence is a blunt instruction to take action on the subject of the article.

Doctor, I feel slightly funny

c) The metaphor 'we're just African apes on the briefest of joyrides' has the effect of putting our lives in perspective in the face of the life of the universe. The whole evolutionary process from ape to man is a mere blink in the face of eternity. Our fate is sealed, so we shouldn't waste time worrying about imaginary ailments, but just get on and enjoy it.

d) The final paragraph is effective because it ends with a plea to the reader to take a lesson from what has gone before. By turning to his own experience and making it personal to the reader by using 'we', the writer concludes that worry does no good and that resources need to be saved for the really ill people. It also recalls the beginning of the article, which stated that the problem was 'too many patients', and the bulk of the article has proved that many of these are not 'patients' at all.

A seatbelt that stops me dozing off at the wheel? Baaa humbug to that

e) This sentence is effective because it allows the writer to move on from the initial experience of the butcher's shop and its risks to the real subject of the article – the new form of seatbelt – designed, supposedly, to reduce risk. It begins to fulfil the promise of the title, which until this point in the article had seemed to be irrelevant.

Section 5 – Summary

Proof at last: being fat is not our fault

1. • The food industry exploits our weakness.
   • Scientific means are used to stimulate our appetites and to condition us to make food addictive.
   • There are methods of fighting back, but because we have to eat it is hard.

Commentary

Although there are four paragraphs, and so you might expect four key points, paragraphs 2 and 3 are saying approximately the same thing – that the industry exploits our psychological and physical systems using scientific methods.

In the first paragraph the topic is set out in the first two sentences. The first sentence on its own is not enough.

BBC is shutting out young Britain

1. • The 'Youth' part of the BBC audience who watch BBC3 are being sidelined because they have no power to make a fuss.
   • For the older and more prosperous BBC audience there is plenty of choice without BBC3.
   • The BBC tried to satisfy all audiences but it can't afford it.
   • Audience figures suggest Radio 4 is less used than BBC3 – but BBC3 will go because its audience has no voice.
   • The young don't have any other alternative, but they will be ignored.
   • The BBC will go on playing to audiences that represent majorities.
   • Young Britain will be disadvantaged by the cut.

2. • The BBC tried to cater for all audiences, but it needs to make cuts.
   • The more powerful majority audiences will continue to be catered for.
   • The 'Youth' section of the BBC's audience is being disadvantaged.

> ## Commentary
>
> When you look at the seven bullet points, you recognise that there are similarities between some of them. If you boiled them down to three or four, that would be a good answer. Five or six points would be too many.

The madness of crowds

1. **Positive:**
   • We need the affection and mutual support that crowds give.
   • We like to belong to a group.
   • Groups were efficient in evolutionary terms in helping us to face dangers.
   • Supporting a football team gives a sense of harmonious togetherness.
   • We should take sides collectively to fight evil.

2. Negative:
   • Crowds can be manipulated into doing horrible things.
   • Football terraces contain two sides, both of whom will not be equally happy about the match result, and that may cause trouble.

> ## Commentary
>
> Questions 1 and 2 ask you to isolate 'fors' and 'againsts'. When you come to the comparison part of the book (Part Three), you will be finding 'fors' and 'againsts' among the points put forward by two different writers.

3. • Not taking sides (impartiality) is a virtue where decisions need to be unbiased.
   • Knowing when to take sides or not to take sides is wisdom.

PART TWO

SINGLE PASSAGES

In this part there are passages and questions modelled on the first part of the exam paper. They will give you a good opportunity to put into practice the skills you learned in Part One. Because these exercises are for practice, the balance between Understanding and Analysis does not necessarily reflect the final exam. Thus Passage A concentrates on Understanding, Passage B introduces more Analysis, while Passage C is a rather quirky example, in which the dominant feature is the writer's tone.

Although the full exam paper has two passages and a comparison question, the questions on Passage 1 are worth 25 of the 30 marks, so it's important that you can cope with them confidently before turning your attention to the comparison question (which will be discussed in Part Three of this book).

At the end of each of the first two passages in this part, however, you will find a 'supplementary question'. This is designed to help you prepare for work on the comparison question in Part Three. There are commentaries and suggested answers for these supplementary questions in the *Answers and Marking Schemes* book.

When answering the questions in this part, you should remember the following points:

- **Identify** means you are looking for 'slices' of information. Then you have to translate these as far as is reasonably possible into your own words.

- **Explain** means you are being asked to show either that you understand the meaning of a particularly complex part of the passage, or that you can see where the argument of the passage is going.

- **Analyse** means you have to show what the effect of a particular use of language is. But you have to be sure what exactly you are being asked to do.

  - 'Analyse how word choice [for example] is effective in …' means that you have to look at word choice – nothing else.
  - 'Analyse how imagery and sentence structure help the writer to …' means you have to look at *both* of these features.
  - 'Analyse how features such as imagery and tone create an effective description of …' means that you may use the two features mentioned, but you don't have to – 'such as' tells you that these are only examples of the kind of features you might find. You could use sentence structure or sound effects or any other feature you think is effective – this is an 'open' list.
  - 'Analyse how the writer's use of language increases your appreciation of …' means that you are free to choose any feature you notice is important. It is helpful to run through your own list of possible features until you find one, or more than one, that you think is effective.

- **Evaluate** means you will be asked to look at the success (or otherwise) of an aspect of the text. For example:

  - A writer's conclusion to a passage is often something you can look at to judge the overall success of the passage in achieving its purpose.
  - There could be a particularly important section of the passage that the writer emphasises in order to clarify your thoughts or stir your emotions or persuade you to accept her ideas. You could be asked to evaluate the success of that portion of the passage.
  - Remember that in evaluation you are free to say 'how far' something is successful – and you could come to the conclusion that it is not successful, but you must support your opinion. You might think, for example, that an image you are being asked about is not particularly effective because it is so overused as to have become a bit of a meaningless cliché.

PASSAGE A

In this passage Joyce McMillan, writing in *The Scotsman* newspaper in February 2013, discusses options for Scotland's future supply of energy.

Read the passage below and attempt the questions that follow.

Fracking

Take the train from Edinburgh to Glasgow – by the northern route through Falkirk, or the southern one through Bathgate – and you find yourself passing through a landscape shaped and still scarred by the huge industrial revolution that swept through central Scotland between 1700 and 1900. There are the coal bings of West Lothian, now grassed
5 over; there are canals and old railway lines, and down on Carron shore near Grangemouth the remains of one of Britain's oldest oil shale industries, and what was once its biggest ironworks.

The sense of having left this industrial past behind us has been a key part of Scotland's changing sense of its own identity over the past 40 years. For good or ill, we seemed to have
10 lost the old, dirty, heavy industries, the coal, steel and shipbuilding that created our hard men and shaped our working-class culture. The work created as part of Glasgow's iconic year as European City of Culture in 1990 was in some ways a long elegy for that past; a coming-to-terms with the idea that we now had to make things new.

15 So we started to imagine a future that would be clean, green and sustainable, built around Scotland's well-deserved image as a beautiful, unspoiled and relatively quiet place, on the northern edge of a crowded continent. And it all seemed, too, to make some kind of economic sense; it's only a few years since international experts were referring to Scotland as a potential 'Saudi Arabia' of the age of renewables, a place so rich in wind, wave and tidal power that we might become world leaders in generating the energy of

20 the future.

In the last half-decade, though, the global energy scene has experienced a sudden and decisive change, thanks to the technology called 'fracking'. The word – short for 'hydraulic fracturing' – must be one of the ugliest in the dictionary; and if the sound is unattractive, the process it describes also seems exceptionally violent. Essentially, it involves the

25 injection of high-pressure water and chemicals deep into underground shale deposits, to break them up and release trapped natural gas. It generates energy that is much cheaper than other fossil fuels or renewables, and is cleaner – in terms of carbon emissions – than coal or oil. And it is widely credited with the recent signs of recovery in the American economy, as the fracking industry drives down energy prices, puts more money in the

30 pockets of American companies and consumers, and creates tens of thousands of jobs wherever it goes.

Now of course it's tempting for those of us who are interested in a decent and sustainable future to dismiss the whole fracking boom as just another symptom of hydrocarbon madness. The long-term impacts of widespread fracking are simply unknown. There seems

35 little chance that the powerful chemicals used in the process, including known carcinogens, will not find their way eventually into ground water sources, polluting them for decades to come; and as for its impact on global warming, it is truly frightening – despite the slightly cleaner carbon profile of shale gas – to think of a planet already on the brink of devastating climate change pouncing so gleefully on yet another source of fossil fuel.

40 Yet when it comes to practical decisions about this new source of energy, it is already clear that there is no chance of humanity turning its back on this new wave of cheap energy; and that truth presents the Scottish Government with a uniquely difficult choice. For by a sharp, ironic twist of history, it seems Scotland is quite rich in shale-gas potential, with the main deposits lying just where the old industrialists of the eighteenth and nineteenth

45 centuries might have guessed they would, along the Forth-Clyde Valley, south towards Dumfries, and north-east towards Fife and Aberdeenshire. According to a report published this week by PricewaterhouseCoopers, the development of fracking could eventually benefit the Scottish economy by up to £5 billion a year; and the whole enterprise is bound to seem tempting to a cash-strapped government, not least because of Scotland's existing

50 expertise in gas and oil technology, and of the danger of being left dependent on imported energy, in a world increasingly fuelled by cheap fracked gas.

It would be unwise, though, for Scotland to plunge into the fracking business without first considering what we lose, in abandoning the dream of a future powered almost entirely by renewables. There is something infinitely attractive about the idea of an economy that

55 is better at conserving energy, less profligate with it, lighter in its touch on the planet, and more certain of its long-term future. The green energy dream is one that fits Scotland's landscape, plays to its unique strengths, and matches the twenty-first-century image it was starting to build for itself; the plunge into fracking and shale-gas exploitation, by contrast, seems in many ways like a return to the past, and we should not discount the

60 psychological cost of making that U-turn.

65 The Government, of course, is likely – in this as in so many other areas – to argue that we can have the best of both worlds, with both fracking and renewable energy in our twenty-first-century power portfolio. Out there in the real world, though, where energy prices are set, the availability of cheap gas worldwide will make investment in expensive renewables schemes less economically attractive by the day. Scotland stands, in other words, at a frightening crossroads between what seems economically unavoidable in the medium term, and what seems right for this country in the long term.

Questions

1. Explain in your own words the key points the writer makes in lines 1–13 about Scotland. — 3
2. Analyse how the writer's word choice in lines 14–20 conveys a positive image of Scotland. — 2
3. Identify in your own words **three** advantages of fracking given in lines 21–31. — 3
4. Identify in your own words **three** possible dangers of fracking given in lines 32–39. — 3
5. Explain why, according to lines 40–51, fracking is 'bound to seem tempting' to the Scottish Government. — 3
6. Re-read lines 52–60.
   a) Identify in your own words **four** advantages of renewable energy given in these lines. — 4
   b) Analyse how the writer's use of language in these lines emphasises the contrast between renewables and fracking. — 4
7. 'Scotland stands ... at a frightening crossroads' (lines 65–66).
   Evaluate the effectiveness of this metaphor as a way of describing the dilemma the Scottish Government faces about fracking. — 3

Supplementary question

Imagine that in the exam the second passage is one that proclaims the virtues of renewable energy sources. The comparison question asks you to identify key areas on which the writers **agree**. Which **two** key ideas would you identify from this first passage?

Answers

Answers can be found in the *Answers and Marking Schemes* book, on pages 2–4.

PASSAGE B

In this passage Katie Grant, writing in *The Scotsman* newspaper, is quite critical of the idea of a gap year, but wonders if it might be a good idea for some Scottish school-leavers.

Read the passage below and attempt the questions that follow.

Gap years

As the mother of a gap-year student, I read with interest extracts of the study 'Seeing the World: An Examination of Backpacking as a Global Youth Culture' by Lucy Huxley, a sociologist at Manchester Metropolitan University. Lucy Huxley may be a clever girl, for all I know, but why it took her three years, and doubtless thousands of taxpayers' pounds, to
5   discover that gap-year students may go abroad but, once there, hang about mostly with each other, phone home constantly and learn almost nothing about the country to which they have travelled, I do not know. Twenty-four hours in the home of a gap-year student's parents would have shown her, more graphically than any study, what modern gap-yearing is all about.

10   In the main, it is about pretence: the pretence of independence. The advent of email has made that pretence increasingly difficult to uphold, but we do it anyway. Since our gap-year daughter is in Italy and unlikely to read this, I will reveal, with a twinge of disloyalty, that scanning back through her emails, I know almost nothing of her life, but an awful lot about her bank account.

15 Recently, as I travelled on the train between Glasgow and Edinburgh, I found myself sitting behind a group of first-year university students indulging in an exquisite (for the listener) game of one-upmanship over their gap-year travels. In those weary, God-I'm-sooooo-cool-I-can-hardly-speak voices, two young men and a young woman talked about bars they had visited in a country whose name seemed to have escaped them – not that it mattered – and
20 how difficult it was to manage a hangover when the temperature was 35°C. They laughed, again in their soooo-cool way, about vomiting in the street of a town (un-named) among people (un-named) who were 'really soooo sweet'.

Then they tried to outdo each other's tales of discomfort. I am sure they thought all their fellow passengers were suitably impressed by their gappie sophistication. Sadly, we were
25 too polite to disabuse them.

These young people illustrated only too clearly that, for most young adults, gap years have become nothing more than a jolly way to kill time. Nowadays, although gappies still return home with that oddly endearing kind of youthful arrogance that declares them to have been there, done that, as if that settled the matter, in fact their year out no longer
30 generates any real knowledge about anything, as the path most of them have trodden is well-beaten and they mostly hang out with each other.

It is claimed that students have a more productive time if they go to countries on organised placements. But whereas this has some advantages, if only to stop gap-year students wandering pointlessly from bar to beach and back, it still does not quite produce the
35 independence of spirit, or the ability to cope with the unexpected, or the severance from the familiar that a gap-year should ideally be all about. If a gap year student's greatest achievement is to have followed the advice of some group leader on a pre-packaged expedition to a specially-made jungle camp, or to have successfully spent some months essentially playing at being a teacher in a Third World village, all arranged through an
40 organisation like Gap Activity Projects, they will have had a wonderful time, and may even have learned a skill or two, but it is hardly the stuff from which heroes are made.

It would be unfair to tar all gappies with the same brush – some do use their time productively – but it seems to me that gap years have forfeited any claim to be an essential part of the maturing process. For middle-class British students, the best that can be
45 said is that a gap year begins, very gently, to wean them away from the culture of the risk assessment exercise and the health and safety checklist that has cosseted them all their lives so far. Though insured to the last strand of designer-straightened hair, gap-year students must, I hope, take at least a smidgen more responsibility for themselves than they did in their school sixth form.

50 I don't want to throw the baby out with the bathwater, however. If, for middle-class English gappies, far from teaching them how to combat loneliness and homesickness or opening their ears and eyes to other cultures, the gap year has become little more than an early introduction to corporate bonding, where the only lesson learned is how much they can drink under a baking sun, there are others who would benefit hugely.

55 When I was at Glasgow University (graduated 1997), far too many of my fellow students had scarcely been beyond the end of the road. The Scottish system, which sees students finishing school one term and beginning 'yooni' the next, in effect simply swapping the classroom for the lecture hall while still living at home and being looked after by their mothers, is as grim a recipe for parochialism of outlook as you could devise.

→

60   There are, I know, good financial reasons for this arrangement, particularly with the four-year Scottish honours degree system. But it sets such a limit on the student's outlook on the world that it should be discouraged. University should be a faintly alarming experience. It should see students feeling, occasionally, that they have leaped out of a plane without a parachute. If Scottish students cannot afford to live away from home

65   during their university careers, a pre-university gap year, however pre-packaged, might provide some useful shock therapy. Moreover, if more Scottish students took a gap year, university dropout rates – currently rising – would drop, since those shovelled into the university system as statistical cannon-fodder would probably realise, as their horizons broadened, that 'yooni' was not for them and find something else to do.

Questions

1. Identify in your own words **two** criticisms made of gap years in lines 1–14.   2
2. Re-read lines 15–31.
   a) Explain in your own words why the writer thinks that the students on the train illustrate the unsatisfactory nature of gap years.   3
   b) Analyse how the writer's use of language in these lines makes fun of the students. In your answer you should refer to such features as word choice, sentence structure and tone.   4
3. Re-read lines 32–41.
   a) Explain in your own words the key criticisms made of 'organised placements'.   2
   b) Analyse how the writer's word choice and sentence structure in these lines make clear her negative view of 'organised placements'.   4
4. Using your own words, identify from lines 42–54 **three** possible advantages of a gap year.   3
5. Re-read lines 55–69.
   a) Using your own words, identify **three** reasons the writer gives for suggesting that a gap year would be good for many Scottish young people.   3
   b) By referring to at least **two** features of language in these lines, analyse how the writer emphasises the points she is making about Scottish school leavers.   4

Supplementary question

Imagine that in the exam the second passage is one in which the writer puts forward many positive points about gap years. The comparison question asks you to identify key areas on which the writers **disagree**. Which **two** key ideas would you identify from this first passage?

Answers

Answers can be found in the *Answers and Marking Schemes* book, on pages 5–8.

PASSAGE C

In this passage Tony Parsons, writing in *GQ* magazine in November 2012, reveals his strong dislike of tattoos.

Read the passage below and attempt the questions that follow.

Tattoos

Twenty years ago, tattoos smacked of the shell suit and the pea brain, the white van and the red-top, the prison yard and Popeye the Sailor Man. Who had tattoos? A bunch of fat thickos
5 and their ropey birds.

Now you will see tattoos languishing around the pool of the five-star hotel or peeking from a fluffy robe at the spa or reaching for the bar nibbles in the Concorde Room at Heathrow
10 (first-class ticket holders only). Now you see tattoos on the great and the good, the rich and famous, all these beautiful people with IQs considerably higher than their shoe size who really should know better than to casually
15 stain themselves with a mark they will carry to the grave.

Tattoos got sexy. Tattoos got cool. Tattoos went mainstream. Tattoos got respectable. Tattoos got middle class. Tattoos became such
20 a widely accepted form of genteel rebellion that even the wife of the prime minister has a discreet little dolphin on her right ankle.

Only one thing did not change: tattoos remained as repulsive as ever.

What happened? How did the British develop this addiction to staining themselves with poorly drawn cartoons?

25 Tattoos were once the province of the rump of the working class – men and women who made a mark on their body because they would never make a mark on their life or the world. That is clearly no longer the case – the richest young men and women in the land are up to their armpits in 'body art' – as if these sub-moronic smears were done by Matisse or Picasso, not some mug with an O Level in art. Tattoos are now sported on people with good
30 degrees and a black AmEx. Now these inky atrocities are just as likely to be seen on upper-middle-class flesh as on someone sucking up the bounty of the welfare state.

→

The very first written reference to tattoos was in 1769. Writing in the ship's diary on the first voyage of Captain Cook, Sir Joseph Banks noted the primitive daubings of Samoan natives: 'I shall now mention the way they mark themselves indelibly, each of them so
35 marked by their humour or disposition.'

No need to journey to the uncharted ends of the world today. No need to sail away for three years to study tribes who cook their food without a microwave. Just go down the Rat and Trumpet on a Friday night. Just go on to a Caribbean beach full of rich white tourists. Just go to Number Ten Downing Street.

40 Two hundred and fifty years ago, tattoos were seen as a sign of the primitive. Now they are perceived as a sign of the enlightened. Tattoos were used as a sign of tribal allegiance – from the Maori of New Zealand to the Picts – 'the painted ones' – of Iron Age Scotland to the natives of the South Seas. And tribal identity is what they still represented 20 years ago.

Now tattoos attempt to represent the antithesis of tribal identity. They are alleged to be an
45 expression of individuality. Yet, all these highly unique individuals who are so special and different have all got exactly the same dopey dolphin or the same martial arts symbol or the same soppy flowers.

Twenty years ago tattoos were about as cool as lager vomit dribbling down a white shell suit. But when the Tattooed Nation gets its dopey little dolphins done, you know they feel
50 cooler than they ever did in their empty lives. But tattoos don't seem cool anymore. They seem lukewarm. They seem ancient.

Who had tattoos when I was a child? My father and Popeye the Sailor Man.

Tattoos signified untamed masculinity, a wild youth and, above all, a life on the ocean waves. My dad had a Fairbairn-Sykes commando knife on one arm, and my mother's
55 name – Emma – on the other. They seemed perfectly natural – my old man had been in the Royal Navy, and then the Royal Naval Commandos. His tattoos did not strike me as particularly shocking or ugly.

What I remember most about my father's tattoos is that they seemed inseparable from his maleness. It wasn't Popeye the Sailor-person, was it? My mother would no more have got a
60 tattoo than she would have eloped with Tom Jones.

The great misconception about tattoos is that they improve anything. David Beckham is handsome, fit and very rich – that is why he is an attractive man, not because he resembles a seagull that fell into an oil slick. Cheryl Cole is a doe-eyed, pretty young woman – her beauty is not derived from the florist's shop that she has forever printed on her bum.

65 Because the rich and famous have embraced tattoos, the middling and the mediocre have embraced them too. Beckham's daubings look bad enough, but how much worse will a tattoo look on somebody with no money, no looks and no muscle tone.

And sometimes tattoos vandalise the skin of those who have nothing but their youth and beauty. At Ascot this year, the enclosure was awash with pretty young women covered
70 in hideously unsightly tattoos. And the tragedy was they all looked so pleased with themselves.

The painted people always react with wild indignation when you cock a dismayed eyebrow at the tattoos. They protest too much. They are not the victims of prejudice; they are just the victims of someone who can't draw very well.

Questions

1. Re-read lines 1–31.
   a) Identify in your own words the key differences the writer sees between the people who had tattoos 20 years ago and those who have them now.   4
   b) By referring to at least two features, analyse how the writer uses language to convey his dislike for tattoos and/or the people who have them. You may wish to refer to such features as word choice, sentence structure and tone.   4
2. 'Now tattoos attempt to represent the antithesis of tribal identity' (line 44).
   By referring in detail to lines 32–47, explain how the writer develops this idea.   4
3. Identify the writer's tone in lines 48–51 and analyse how it is conveyed.   3
4. By referring to lines 52–60, explain in your own words why the writer thinks his father's tattoos were acceptable.   3
5. Identify in your own words **three** key points the writer makes about tattoos in lines 61–71.   3
6. Evaluate the effectiveness of the final paragraph (lines 72–74) as a conclusion to the passage as a whole. You should refer in your answer to ideas and tone.   4

Answers

Answers can be found in the *Answers and Marking Schemes* book, on pages 9–12.

PART THREE

COMPARISON

This skill is (like summary) a really important aspect of your ability to read effectively. The ability to compare two views, to detect bias or to make an informed decision as to which course of action to take, is really important in the 'real' world – as distinct from the 'examination' world. The passages in this part of the book are designed to offer you chances to practise comparative tasks. You will find the work you have done on evaluation and summary (Part One Sections 4 and 5) very helpful in these exercises.

This part of the book is divided into three sections:

- Section 1 contains advice and exercises involving short passages, looking at various ways of tackling this kind of question.

- Section 2 moves on to full-length passages but there is still some support in dealing with the tasks.

- Section 3 presents full-length passages for comparison, allowing scope for the practice of the skills developed throughout the previous two sections.

SECTION 1 – SHORT PASSAGES

The comparative evaluation of texts is the last task facing you in a Reading for Understanding, Analysis and Evaluation paper.

By the time you get to this question, you will already have worked your way through the questions on Passage 1, so you will be fairly familiar with the ideas in it.

You will have made notes of some kind on Passage 2, trying to isolate key points by using the methods practised in Part One.

Comparing, at its simplest, involves identifying where the writers agree and where they disagree about the topic.

There are two parts to a typical comparison question. The first part asks you to:

Identify key areas on which the writers agree (or disagree).

The second part states:

In your answer, you should refer in detail to both passages.

There is practice in identifying key areas in Part One in Section 5 Summary.

It is probable that there will be only three or four really important points to identify, and you should concentrate on these.

You have to learn to distinguish the key idea from such things as definitions, illustrations, examples and expansions, which are there to support the key idea. On some occasions the topic sentence will help you towards the important area in a paragraph, but in longer passages not all paragraphs will be of equal importance. You can find information about all these ideas on pages 39–41.

The following exercise allows you to practise these skills on very short and quite simple passages. The layout in two columns helps because you can compare across or join similar ideas between the two columns, and the passages are still very short compared with what you will be asked to do later.

A. Celebrity talent shows

The revelation of the guests for the latest runs of two celebrity talent contests suggests a definite shift in personnel. Rory Bremner becomes
5   the first practising satirist to sign up for *Strictly Come Dancing*, while Kirsty Wark is the first serving current affairs heavyweight to tackle *Celebrity MasterChef*.
10   When the star challenge genre took off (with *Celebrity Big Brother* and

➡

B. *Strictly Come Dancing* – TV media blog

It would surely be dream casting for the BBC if Pippa Middleton were to slip on her dancing shoes and join the raggletaggle of celebrities taking part
5   in *Strictly Come Dancing*. And according to reports, producers of the Beeb's ballroom behemoth have approached the Duchess of Cambridge's sister to do just that.

➡

I'm a Celebrity…), it was generally
regarded as a sort of welfare state
or pension scheme for the neglected
15   or semi-retired. The perception was
that failing at trivial challenges might
damage the credibility of a serious
journalist or actor. Being exposed as
the worst public dancer since David
20   Brent turned John Sergeant into a
light entertainment celebrity (*The One
Show*, ITV documentaries), but would
have finished him if he had still been
a political editor.

25   Now, though, a class system of talent
franchises has become established.
While the London house-share and
the Aussie jungle are still considered
below the top tier of celebrity society,
30   *Strictly Come Dancing* and *MasterChef*
are viewed as toff slots, with the
possession of a hot trot or knock-out
risotto suggesting breadth of character.

Regardless of how far they get in the
35   contests, Bremner and Wark should
still be able to go back to lampooning
and interviewing government
ministers, although there must be
a slight risk of a cheeky politician
40   saying: 'Kirsty, that question is as thick
and tasteless as your peach pavlova.'

So the spirit of Comic Relief – in
which serious TV types show what
sports they are by doing something
45   silly or unexpected – has now spread
across the schedules. The judgements
are delicate. There are still people
whose broadcasting credibility could
not easily survive – Jeremy Paxman,
50   Ian Hislop, David Dimbleby – but, as
Wark and Bremner have realised,
there are now designated green zones
for upmarket stars who want to
sashay or sauté competitively.

Mark Lawson in *The Guardian*

10   Amid copious references to her
posterior ('It's *Strictly* bum dancing',
'Pert Pippa's not-so-bum deal',
and the like), *The Sun* has claimed
the future queen-in-law has been
15   offered 'a five-figure sum', because
clad in skimpy sequinned costumes,
P-Middy would boost ratings – not
to mention send tabloid hacks
scurrying for the 'buttock' section
20   of their thesauruses regardless
of where she'd finish on the
leaderboard. (Bottom, obviously.)

This got us thinking – who else
would we like to see being insulted
25   by Craig Revel Horwood under a
glitterball in three months' time?
There's nothing *Strictly* likes more
than a serious, suity type letting
their hair down and it's proved a
30   fertile career boost for some serious
broadcast journalists, notably
'dancing pig' John Sergeant. Who
could step out from behind their
desk next? Anna Ford's got the
35   legs, Jon Snow's taste in ties might
indicate latent Latin flair, and
Sir Trevor McDoughnut would go
down well.

There are invariably some sportsmen,
40   and Manchester United's Gary
Neville and Edwin van der Sar are
newly retired – although we'd rather
see their team-mate Ryan Giggs
struggling to stick to one partner.

45   But that's enough twinkle-toed
speculation from us. Do you fancy
watching Pippa's paso doble? Who
would you like to see whirling,
twirling and tolerating Brucie's dad-
50   jokes come September? Let us know
below. And, it almost goes without
saying, keeeeeep dancing.

Michael Hogan in *The Guardian*

Passage A is concerned with whether or not taking part in celebrity shows damages the reputation of serious presenters and TV journalists. It talks about how such shows used to be viewed – and how some of them are still not respectable – but it comes down in the end to recognising that serious TV personalities can engage in certain shows without losing their credibility.

Passage B talks of a number of kinds of contestants who might take part in such shows – footballers, semi-royals, serious broadcast journalists – but the **only** paragraph that has any relevance to the question you have been asked is the third paragraph, which introduces the idea that serious journalists do not damage their careers by taking part.

Task

The subject is television celebrity talent shows.

● Identify one key area on which the writers agree.
● In your answer, you should refer in detail to both passages.

Answer

● The writers agree that serious TV commentators can now take part in certain of these celebrity shows without losing their position as responsible reporters and interviewers.

You can write your answer as above, in continuous prose, or you can use developed bullet points – although in this case only one bullet point is required:

● Serious commentators can take part in celebrity shows without damaging their careers.

Referring in detail to both passages:

● The writer of Passage A says that Wark and Bremner can both go back to serious broadcasting, commentating on serious politics.
● The writer of Passage B talks about 'suity types' (serious journalists like Jon Snow and John Sergeant) whose careers would flourish.

(It is possible that you can see a little disagreement between the two writers about the effect on John Sergeant's career, but you weren't asked about any differences, so you don't mention them.)

The next exercise is closer to one you might find in the exam, but the passages are still short and the question asks for **two** key areas only.

Exercise 1 – Does man flu really exist?

Yes

I was introduced to 'man flu' by the actor Nick Frost. He was lying on a sofa at the time, wrapped in a dressing gown and looking decidedly
5   peaky. He had it. Paramedics were called and a bell given to him with which he could summon his perplexed girlfriend for brow-mopping and channel-changing.

10   Like all men, I had been laid low with 'man flu' on many occasions. But this was the first time I had heard it talked about openly. It may only have been a comedy show, but someone ➜

No

So Cambridge University researchers propose that evolution has left men more susceptible to the sniffles than women. Was this study led by a man,
5   perchance? Of all the evolutionary theories I have heard, this is the most ridiculous. Are we seriously to believe that the exaggerated moans that characterise man flu can be put down
10   to the fact that men's Neanderthal tendencies have left them with weaker immune systems? It would be more believable if scientists had pronounced the existence of ➜

15 was taking man flu seriously at last. The fightback, I thought, has begun.

It wasn't Frost who came up with the name 'man flu', because no man would give to this serious affliction 20 such a trite and obviously sarcastic name. But whoever it was, she obviously hasn't been keeping up with the advances in evolutionary biology. If she had, she might have 25 been following more closely the work of Cambridge University's Dr Olivier Restif.

Last week, he revealed what Nick Frost, me and all other blokes have 30 always known – that 'man flu' is real and fully undeserving of those oh-so-sceptical inverted commas. That's real as in 'not a figment of our imaginations, but a medically 35 proven fact'.

Okay, here's the science bit. I'll keep it simple so the distaff side of *The Herald* readership can follow it. Basically, men are pre-programmed to do 40 foolhardy stuff like buy motorbikes and eat black pudding because we need a competitive edge in the old baby-making stakes. It's something to do with testosterone, apparently.

45 Unfortunately, this function results in a deficit in another part of our make-up, in this case, the immune system. In short, ours don't work as well as yours, ladies. When we're exposed to 50 nasty viruses we're far less able to deal with them. And so we get what is sneeringly referred to as 'man flu'.

Whatever we call it, it should no longer be an excuse for sarcasm or 55 disinterest from wives, girlfriends or mothers. Instead, it should be indulged, preferably with sympathy, soup and (most importantly) possession of the TV remote. And if 60 you hear a bell ringing, girls, stick the kettle on.

Barry Didcock in *The Herald*

15 a malingering gene – one that prompted a pathetic display of whining and the need for pandering in response.

Women haven't time for self-20 indulgent cries for sympathy. While we're busy multi-tasking, there's little time left at the end of a day for so much as a soak in the tub, let alone a few days off wallowing in 25 self-pity. For most women – mothers especially – the only option, rather than watch the dishes pile up and the children go hungry, is to grin and bear it. Where women downplay, 30 men exaggerate. For them, a cold is the flu, a headache is a migraine.

This tendency towards exaggeration can be put down to ego. Men, for all their bravado and machismo, like to 35 be cared for and fussed over.

But it's not their fault. I blame their mothers. Having received attention and sympathy from their mums all their lives, men expect this as a norm 40 from women – particularly their partners. I can almost guarantee that man flu is more prevalent in men who have girlfriends or wives – that is, someone available to look 45 after them.

Man flu is a clever ploy – whether subconscious or not – to garner sympathy and take time off to watch old footie videos while calling 50 in maid service. But we must, on no account, sisters, give in to their whining. Let them sniff and get on with it.

Ali Howard in *The Herald*

Question

Identify two key areas on which the writers disagree. In your answer, you should refer in detail to both passages.

To answer this, you have to follow the steps:

1. Write down, in your own words, the two key areas of disagreement you have identified.
2. Then provide evidence from the passages for your choice of each of these key areas.

Your evidence might take the form of quotations from the passages that you link with the key idea concerned, or your evidence might be in the form of an explanation of how certain parts of the passage led you to your conclusions about the key areas.

Answer

The answer can be found in the *Answers and Marking Schemes* book, on page 13.

The next example is slightly longer, and not set out in columns, so that your note taking will be more difficult. You should experiment with various ways of identifying similar key ideas. Writing brief notes for yourself in two columns might help, or possibly using highlighters, or numbering key points.

Exercise 2 – CCTV in schools

Passage 1

Research on CCTV cameras in schools estimates that there are now more than 100,000 CCTV cameras in secondary schools and academies across England, Scotland and Wales.

My concerns about the scale of their use are not only a matter of the privacy of school children and teachers, but are also over the reasons why Britain continues to race ahead
5 of nearly every other country when it comes to surveillance.

All too often, surveillance is used as a quick fix, with little or no evaluation of whether it actually addresses the problem. Does it really reduce bullying, or does it displace it? Would better lockers be a more effective way to reduce theft? Numerous reports looking at CCTV have found it does little to deter crime. One report in 2007 looking at Parisian
10 schools found that CCTV was 'at best ineffective, at worst negative'. Theft continued to increase and intruders were not prevented from entering the premises.

It seems prudent to establish an evidential basis before pursuing such widespread surveillance, particularly given the heightened sensitivity of recording young people at school. Indeed, some teachers have been making strong arguments about how they
15 believe CCTV undermines the relationship they have with their pupils and that it is not a prerequisite of a safe school.

Parents, teachers and pupils need to be part of the discussion. The Government has a role to play too. Unfortunately, the Home Office's proposed regulatory system – a code of practice and a new surveillance camera commissioner – is far too weak to give anyone
20 real confidence that oversight of CCTV cameras is robust. The code will not directly apply to schools, while the commissioner will have no powers of inspection or enforcement. We think the code should apply to all publicly funded organisations, and that the commissioner should have those powers. It would be ridiculous if, in a situation where a parent, teacher or pupil feels a camera is intrusive, the person responsible for overseeing
25 surveillance cameras was not able to investigate and take any action necessary.

Combined with evidential studies into how CCTV is being used and whether it is actually improving safety, I believe that we can ensure any surveillance in schools is proportionate and absolutely necessary.

Nick Pickles in *The Guardian*

Passage 2

We have 162 CCTV cameras at St Mary's. The teachers, governors and parents all feel that they make a significant contribution to the safeguarding of our students and staff and help to protect property. There are 18 cameras located in each of the school's toilet suites. They are focused on basin areas and are very overt. Children tell us this is one of
5 the areas of the school where they are concerned about potential bullying. Other cameras are located in specialist rooms for teaching ICT and technology, where there is expensive equipment such as computers and laser cutters, in general circulation areas and in areas deemed to be high risk for theft, such as cycle racks, or for ingress by trespassers such as the entrance way.

10 The cameras are not used as part of a surveillance system. Tapes are only viewed by me or another senior member of staff if there is an incident, in order to confirm who is responsible. In the almost three years since the cameras have been installed there have been two incidents in the toilet suites that involved a little bit of damage; one involved toilet paper being used to block the sink. Across the whole of the school there have only
15 been another two incidents, including an external attempt to steal lead from the roof. In this case, police had access to the CCTV footage and it led to a prosecution.

The number of cameras installed in the school complies with the guidance we received from the Government and the local authority when the new building was completed in 2010. It was designed to support a school population of 1100. We will grow to this
20 population by 2016; now we have 820 pupils so we have a high camera-to-pupil ratio.

One of the important factors parents consider when choosing a school for their children is their child's safety. The feedback from parents about the CCTV cameras has been overwhelmingly positive. I am not aware of any parent who has raised concerns about the possibility of their child being under surveillance or the issue that surveillance becomes
25 the norm. They see the cameras when they visit the school and when I explain that they are part of our safeguarding measures I have only ever received nods of approval. Students are also positive about the cameras. They tell us they feel very safe at school.

Stephanie Benbow in *The Guardian*

Question

Identify key areas on which the writers disagree. In your answer you should refer in detail to both passages.

Hint

Use the practice you had in Part One Section 5 Summary (page 37 especially) to make quick notes about each paragraph. The first passage is done for you:

- Lots of cameras.
- Too much surveillance.
- Cameras don't cut crime.
- Undermines relationships between pupils and staff.
- Regulations too weak, parents might object to surveillance.
- Need evidence to prove it's necessary.

Answer

The answer can be found in the *Answers and Marking Schemes* book, on page 14.

Exercise 3 – JFK

The last example is a slightly longer one for you to try without any extra support.

Passage 1

These days, it is only the world's grandparents who can tell you where they were when they heard John F. Kennedy was dead. For decades that was a staple of the global collective
5   memory, a question that could be asked in Berlin or London as readily as New York or Los Angeles. That memory, despite its age, is going strong. While some presidents, including those who occupied the White House for a full eight
10 years, have struggled to be remembered at all 50 years after their deaths, Kennedy continues to loom large.

Interest in JFK peaks for an anniversary, especially a big one. But the truth is, it hardly
15 ever wanes. What explains this enduring grip on both the public and political imagination?

For one thing, he was that rare politician able to inspire. There's no use pretending that sex and glamour were not at the heart of this. JFK looked young, vigorous and handsome,
20 with a beautiful wife to match. Stark was the contrast with both his predecessors in the Oval Office and his counterparts abroad. He appeared like a new leader for a new era.

That image has endured far beyond the archive footage. Kennedy established a template for political leadership that is still in place, in America and around the world. Kennedyesque is still the style, the demeanour, to which candidates for high office aspire:
25 slim, energetic, accompanied by a supremely elegant spouse.

Of course, much of it was fake. Unknown to the voting public, their fit young president was, in fact, crippled with back pain from Addison's disease, taking industrial quantities of drugs to get through the day. Equally concealed were his serial infidelities, his affairs with women ranging from 19-year-old interns to Marilyn Monroe.

30 Yet none of this seems to diminish the Kennedy legend; it only enhances it. For JFK, the first president of the TV age who understood and exploited the medium, remains, even in death, a celebrity. He is the hero of a story that has everything: sex, lies, gossip, intrigue and lust – all set against a background of peace and war.

What's more, all that is combined with something that is, perhaps, as powerful as sex:
35 hope. Despite everything, the Kennedy brand still stands for idealism – for the ambition of the Moon landing and the call to public service enshrined in one of his most popular programmes, the Peace Corps.

Celebrity and hope: it's a powerful, quintessentially American combination. Fifty years ago the man who embodied it was gunned down. But the myth lives on.

Jonathan Freedland in *The Guardian*

Passage 2

Fifty years after John F. Kennedy's assassination, he remains an object of almost universal admiration. And yet, particularly this year, his legacy has aroused the ire of debunkers who complain that Kennedy is unworthy of all this adulation.

…

5 He was, they say, all image and no substance, a shallow playboy whose foreign policy mistakes and paltry legislative record undermine any claim to greatness. His assassination, personal attributes of good looks and charm, joined to Jacqueline Kennedy's promotion of a Camelot myth, have gone far to explain his popularity.

Such criticism not only gives short shrift to Kennedy's real achievements as a domestic and foreign policy leader, but it also fails to appreciate the presidency's central role:
10 to inspire and encourage the country to move forward, a role that Kennedy performed better than any president in modern memory.

The litany of complaints against Kennedy is a long one. Critics scoff at his image as a devoted family man: They complain that he was as Timothy Noah wrote in The New Republic, 'a compulsive, even pathological adulterer,' whose reckless self-indulgence
15 threatened to destroy his presidency.

…

But Kennedy's greatest success was the very thing that critics often cast as a shortcoming: his charisma, his feel for the importance of inspirational leadership and his willingness to use it to great ends.

Kennedy saw the presidency as the vital center of government, and a president's primary
20 goal as galvanising commitments to constructive change. He aimed to move the country and the world toward a more peaceful future, not just through legislation but through inspiration.

Kennedy's presidential ambitions rested on his understanding of what Washington, Jefferson, Lincoln and F.D.R. had done. Like them, he relied on the spoken word, but he had the advantage of television in reaching millions of people around the globe. And like
25 those predecessors, he saw the need for actions that gave meaning to his rhetoric.

The requests in his Inaugural Address – for Americans to put their country ahead of their selfish concerns and to peoples everywhere to join in a new quest for peace – found substance in the Peace Corps and the Alliance for Progress. His call in May 1961 for a manned mission to the Moon and his 'peace speech' in June 1963 urging Americans to re-examine their attitude
30 toward the Soviet Union were aimed at promoting national unity and international accord.

Compared with other recent presidents whose stumbles and failures have assaulted the national self-esteem, memories of Kennedy continue to give the country faith that its better days are ahead. That's been reason enough to discount his limitations and remain enamoured of his presidential performance.

Robert Dallek in *The New York Times*

Question

Identify key areas on which the writers agree about JFK. In your answer you should refer in detail to both passages.

Answer

The answer can be found in the *Answers and Marking Schemes* book, on pages 14–15.

In this section you will find longer passages, similar to those you will face in the examination. Some questions and tasks will guide you through the passages and prepare you for dealing with the exam-type comparison question at the end of each exercise.

Answers

Answers for the exercises in this section can be found in the *Answers and Marking Schemes* book, on pages 16–19.

Exercise 4 – The First World War

The following two passages were both published in national newspapers on 5 August 2014. They focus on the writers' thoughts the day after the hundredth anniversary of Britain's declaration of war on Germany in 1914.

The writers are broadly in agreement. As you read each passage make notes under the following headings:

- Coverage in the media

- The real horrors of war

- Writer's attitude to the commemorations

- Have lessons been learned?

Passage 1

Britain's commemoration of the Great War has lost all sense of proportion. It has become a media theme park, an indigestible cross between *Downton Abbey* and a horror movie. I cannot walk down the street or turn on the television without being bombarded by Great War diaries, poems, scrapbooks and songs. The BBC has gone war mad. We have Great War
5   plays, Great War proms, Great War bake-ins, Great War gardens, even Great War *Countryfile*. There is the Great War and the Commonwealth, the Great War and feminism, Great War fashion shows and souvenirs. There are reportedly 8000 books on the war in print. The Royal Mail has issued 'classic, prestige and presentation' packs on the war that 'enable you to enjoy both the stories and the stamps'. Enjoy?

10   This has been going on all year. When in January I apologised to German friends for the impending avalanche of anti-German memorabilia, I little realised how great that avalanche would be. A Martian might think Britain was a country of demented warmongers, not able to get through a day without a dose of appalling battle scenes from past national victories. Yesterday the fact that Britain went to war with Germany in 1914 actually led
15   the morning news.

➜

Clearly events of the magnitude of a war should be remembered. But when those who fought and suffered are all dead, 'remembering' is a task for the intellect and imagination. It is essentially work for historians, but we have to pump up 'human interest' in it, especially for children, with tales of personal distress and terrible cruelty. The repetition
20 of virtually identical 'stories from the trenches' becomes banal, a nightly pornography of violence.

The war was terrible, as are all wars. The soldiers who experienced Napoleon's march on Moscow or the soldiers who fought on the Russian front in the Second World War would have regarded the trenches as easy going. Besides, the actual outbreak of a war is by no
25 means its most significant moment, which surely attaches to its completion. No one in 1914 thought they were marching off to 'the Great War', but rather to drive the Germans back over their border by Christmas.

The most sensible commemoration of any war is not to repeat it. Hence, presumably, the constant references by this week's celebrants to 'drawing lessons' and 'lest we forget'. But
30 this is mere cliché if no lessons are then drawn, or if drawn are then forgotten.

The Great War centenary should indeed have been a festival of lessons. Historians have had a field day arguing over its enduring puzzle – not its conduct or its outcome, but its cause. I have come close to changing my mind with each book I have read, veering from Chris Clark's cobweb of treaties and tripwires, to the majority view that firmly blames the
35 Kaiser and Germany. But I have read precious few lessons.

The truth is that Britain is as bad as America at learning from old wars. The American defence secretary during the Vietnam War, Robert McNamara, remarked that every lesson learned from Vietnam was ignored in the invasion of Iraq. In the past decade Britain has waged three unprovoked wars – on Afghanistan, Iraq and Libya – at a vast cost in lives
40 and destruction, and no obvious benefit to anyone. The invasion of Afghanistan ignored the lesson of all previous conflicts in the region and is duly being lost. The truth is that 'drawing lessons' has become code for celebrating victory.

Simon Jenkins in *The Guardian*

Passage 2

During a busy day of TV scheduling devoted to remembering the Great War, the irony was that no one was left who truly remembered. Here was a conflict that killed millions, destroyed the global economy and altered the world for ever, but we had little left to grip in 2014 except some grainy footage, some sad notes from young lads to their mothers, and
5 some nice royals and dignitaries holding flowers.

The bullets, the bloodshed, this futile massacre of life, could only be pieced together second-hand via veterans' children, love-letters from the front, or Chelsea Pensioners recounting the supper-time anecdotes of long-dead friends, who, we were told, would 'sometimes reminisce' about their time 'waiting to die' in the trenches, fearing the whistle that would
10 send them into German fire.

Yet one got the feeling, as another outside broadcast unit in another corner of the Commonwealth picked the brains of another proud son or daughter, that this had been a war fought by tight-lipped, dignified blokes who'd not wanted to talk much about their battle if they were lucky enough to survive.

15 On *Good Morning Britain*, Ben Shephard was knee-deep in a *Who Do You Think You Are?*-style history quest, uncovering the work of his great-grandfather with the Royal Army Medical Corps. 'It was still a dangerous role. I mean, they were dodging chunks of shell like this,' the historian stressed, lugging a large jagged artefact, as big as a football, into shot. Suddenly I understood the actual horror of 'shelling'.

20 Sombre moments like this were scattered throughout the day: Prince Harry in Folkestone, unveiling a memorial arch to symbolise all the lads who marched to the harbour, boarded boats and never returned; the mesmerising sea of ceramic poppies that make up the installation by Paul Cummins outside the Tower of London; Robert Hall's BBC News report on 17-year-old Private John Parr, the first British soldier to lose his life.

25 On Sky News no solemn dignitary, or bow-headed royal representative, went unmonitored. This was the day we got our full money's worth out of our royalty. In Glasgow, the Prince of Wales, dressed in the uniform of a British Admiral of the Fleet, attended the Service of Remembrance at Glasgow Cathedral that featured 1400 invited guests, including representatives of Commonwealth countries, senior military figures and charities.

30 What, I found myself thinking, is the exact point of this grand fuss acknowledging the First World War's horror, when the remaining news headlines proved that not one iota about the unspeakable pointless carnage of war had been learned? Statistics of 1914's fatalities, financial expenditure and subsequent escalation merged with modern-day news of fighting in Gaza, fighting in Libya, fighting in Syria.

35 Then the screen filled with the Prime Minister saying: 'A hundred years ago today, Britain entered the First World War, and we are marking that centenary to honour those who served, to remember those who died, and to ensure that the lessons learned live with us for ever.' The specific lessons any human beings had learned were not expounded on.

Grace Dent in *The Independent*

Now: Re-write your notes in a more organised way, trying to make general points about what the writers are saying about each key area. Try to generalise; if you're using quotations, keep them short.

Finally: Use your re-organised notes to construct an answer to the following exam-type question:

Question

Both writers express their views about the commemoration of the outbreak of the First World War. Identify key areas on which they agree. In your answer, you should refer in detail to both passages.

You may answer this question in continuous prose or in a series of developed bullet points.

Exercise 5 – Serving on a jury

The following passages both appeared in *The Independent* newspaper, the second one eight days after the first. The first passage was written by Matthew Lewin, a writer and journalist; the second by Mark Steel, a newspaper columnist and stand-up comedian.

The passages discuss the writers' experiences of serving on a jury in England. It should be noted the word 'barrister' is the English term for what in Scotland is called an 'advocate'; that is, the lawyer who presents cases to a jury – which in Scotland has 15 members, not 12.

Read both passages straight through and be prepared to answer the question that follows, which will ask you to: **Identify very briefly the key difference of opinion about the jury system**.

Passage 1

'Jury service? Don't worry, it will renew your faith in the jury system,' my friend assured me. But, two weeks and three trials later, I have emerged from a London crown court with my faith in our court system – and in my fellow jurors – severely battered.

5   For a start, as we gathered at 9 a.m. on a foul and rainy Monday morning, there was a distinct shortage of the middle classes on display. Just about everyone with any means, commitments, high-profile or important jobs, and professionals such as doctors and dentists, architects and the like, seemed to have won deferment or exemption from the process. What was left was the proverbial salt of the earth – just the sort of ordinary, sensible people that, you might think, you would want on your jury if you had been unjustly

10   accused of a crime. The trouble was that they also included an inordinate number of people who did not speak English very well, and had serious trouble filling out the simplest forms and understanding the clearest instructions.

The vast majority had never seen the inside of a courtroom; nothing intrinsically wrong with that, I suppose, for why should they have if they had never been a witness or a defendant?

15   The trouble was, however, that most of their knowledge and expectations seemed to have been acquired from watching television's distorted concepts of courtroom procedure. Faced with the real thing, many jurors started drowning in the complexities.

Walking back to the tube station one evening, I was accosted by a fellow juror, a young woman around 25 years old, who asked me: 'Are we supposed to be considering our verdicts

20   tonight?'

'No,' I replied in amazement, 'we haven't heard the case for the defence yet.'

'What's that?' she asked.

The next day I watched her as the adversarial court system began finally to dawn on her consciousness with the defence case, the summings up by barristers and the

25   judge's directions.

I was appalled at how many people on the three juries I sat on neglected to take notes – something that didn't stop most of them from 'remembering' volubly (but erroneously) in the jury room what witnesses, defendants, barristers and the judge had said in court. And, of course, they forgot huge tracts of evidence, no matter how crucial.

30   I was also shocked by how many of the jurors I sat with appeared to have no analytical ability whatsoever; no facility for ordering facts they heard, organising evidence in their minds or applying a kind of sequential logic to opinion – and decision-making – along the lines of 'If this is true … then that must follow.' and 'If we believe A then we can also believe B, and vice versa.' Instead, jurors seemed to reach for facts and opinions in a totally

35   random, haphazard way, seldom relating their views to any consistent approach to the body of evidence they had heard.

But what dismayed me most of all was the number of jurors who had clearly arrived with their own agendas – the main one being a deep distrust of any form of authority and a thinly disguised antagonism to anyone in a police uniform. In all three juries

40   there seemed to be a few hardliners who were on a mission to acquit, and refused to convict no matter how damning the evidence. (Most defendants in film and television courtroom dramas are innocent and fighting to clear their sullied names, so why should real life be any different?) In two cases out of my three they prevailed to some degree, forcing the jury into majority verdicts and in one case forcing the jury to

45   adopt a poor compromise that the judge later described as 'extremely generous' to the accused man.

→

Solutions? Well, I am not suggesting that juries be screened for intelligence, education or prejudice – a process that would run contrary to the concept of a jury being a random selection of one's peers. (And, in any case, who exactly would do the screening?) But,
50 in the short term, something really has to be done to reduce the incidence of able, well educated people avoiding jury service and thereby distorting the mix of abilities on the jury panels.

And I am convinced that there needs to be better training for jurors – better than the brief and partially inaudible video presentation that we saw on the morning we arrived. There
55 has to be a proper induction process, possibly on the Friday before jury service begins, which should include a visit to a courtroom and being given a thorough explanation – perhaps with a bit of role playing by jurors – of court processes and the kind of thinking that should be applied.

Everyone remembers the classic film *Twelve Angry Men*, in which a lone juror, played by
60 Henry Fonda, bravely holds on to his convictions and, in the process, saves an innocent man from being convicted. The film I would make would be called *Twelve Stupid Citizens*, and would show deeply ignorant people acquitting obviously guilty criminals.

Passage 2

I've been fascinated by the letters to *The Independent* discussing jury experiences in light of Matthew Lewin's recent article. Best of all was the reader who complained that the whole system was flawed because his co-jurors spent all day trying to complete a crossword. Can this be entirely accurate? Surely even a judge would notice if, halfway through a witness's
5   evidence, the jury was squabbling over whether the Seine or the Rhine was the one that went through Germany. Maybe the judge thought that, as it was the last day of the trial, the jury should be allowed to bring in games.

What seemed to annoy the letter-writer most was that although it was called a 'coffee-break crossword', it took them all day to finish it, thus proving we're entrusting justice to
10   idiots. Perhaps, instead of being able to replace individual jurors before a trial, a defendant should be able to make an entire jury do a 'fastest-on-the-buzzer' test, like on *Who Wants to Be a Millionaire*. Then your verdict is decided by the one who puts four famous buildings in the right order of height in 4.6 seconds.

I was once on jury service, and felt certain my co-jurors would vote to convict the timid
15   teenage Nigerian defendant, as two police officers had witnessed him selling dope, and he had several chunks in his pocket, which he'd claimed was for his personal use. But the officers contradicted themselves over several details, and one officer said he'd heard the defendant talk to a Spanish couple in Italian, except for the one English sentence, 'I want to sell you some hash'.

20   At that point, I wondered how to calculate exactly how many errors, logically, linguistically and philosophically, were contained in that one piece of evidence, especially as neither of the other officers mentioned this incident at all. Nonetheless, I felt bad for the multilingual dope boy, especially when I saw the juror on my left, a stern woman with the face of a Victorian headmistress – a hanger and flogger for sure. We were sent off to consider our
25   verdict, with the judge's advice: 'You must use your own life experience.'

As soon as we arrived in our little room, I saw that every juror had taken their responsibility incredibly seriously. Everyone had taken notes, listened intensely throughout, and was eager to clarify areas of confusion.

30 I suggested the police evidence was flawed, and gave a couple of examples. Then a woman bus driver gave better examples, and a nurse did the same. So the advertising executive asked if anyone at all believed the police evidence, and the Victorian headmistress said brusquely: 'As far as I'm concerned, the police were telling a pack of lies.' One by one, everybody agreed, so the foreman said: 'Well there's no point in discussing that part of the case at all then.' Then the advertising executive methodically laid out the rest of the case. I
35 wondered whether he was going to come up with a nifty slogan, like: 'The evidence mounts that he's not sold an ounce.'

The one issue remaining was why he had several chunks of dope, having apparently spent all his money. 'Well,' said an architect, 'it's no more strange than someone going to France for two months' worth of wine. He was just stocking up.' A teenage girl said: 'I've
40 sometimes blown all my wages in one go on a pair of shoes. He's just done it with dope.' And an endearing Jamaican pensioner said: 'I've seen men in the music business smoke that much in one afternoon. There, the judge told me to use my life experience, so that's what I've done.'

That is part of the beauty of the jury system. A judge has a life experience entirely alien
45 to that of most people who are tried. Just as obvious is that when people are given a chance to make decisions that have a real impact, they almost all respond with inspiring enthusiasm. In a jury, your voice genuinely counts, your decision has an impact and it will be acted upon, so it's almost the opposite of a vote in a general election. Which is why, in a jury, no one ever says: 'Oh, I can't be bothered to vote. Guilty, not guilty, it doesn't make
50 any difference; all those verdicts are as bad as each other.'

It took us 45 minutes to find the lad not guilty – unanimously. As we all left the court, the nurse, whose name I never knew, said: 'I think we did a good thing today,' and I skipped to the underground station, exhilarated by the humanity of these 11 strangers.

First: Identify very briefly the key difference of opinion about the jury system between the two passages.

Now: To help you identify further points of disagreement, draw up a table similar to the one below and complete it with appropriate details.

	Matthew Lewin		Mark Steel	
	Opinion	Evidence	Opinion	Evidence
The experience of serving on a jury				
Their fellow jurors in general				
Social spread of fellow jurors				
Attitude to the accused				

Then: Add one (or more than one) more row to the left-hand column of the table and fill in the relevant details.

Finally: Use the material you have gathered about the passages to write a structured response to the following exam-type question:

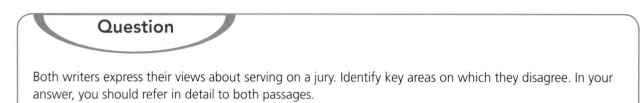

Question

Both writers express their views about serving on a jury. Identify key areas on which they disagree. In your answer, you should refer in detail to both passages.

You may answer this question in continuous prose or in a series of developed bullet points.

Exercise 6 – Competitive sport

The following two passages appeared in national newspapers (*The Herald* and *The Scotsman*) and were written by Jackie Kemp and Gillian Bowditch respectively.

Both writers discuss the subject of competitive sport for young people.

Read both passages straight through and be prepared to answer the question that follows, which will ask you to: **Identify very briefly the key point of similarity in the writers' attitude to competitive sport for young people**.

Passage 1

Say 'school sports day' and memories come flooding back: the rough hessian sack tugged up to the oxters, feet straining at the seams as you waddled, hobbled or leapt across the field, the tie knotted tightly round two small ankles, the smell of hard-boiled egg, shell smashing as it fell off the spoon, the excitement of inter-house or team rivalry, the strangeness of
5   parents being there looking on, and the occasional (in my case, very occasional) delight of getting to wear a winner's ribbon. In 12 years at school, I have a vague memory of once making third in the wheelbarrow race.

As well as the silly races, there were athletics, children running full tilt, hearts thudding in their chests as they pelted towards the finish line. Ancient trials of strength and skill,
10   they were absorbing to watch and even those eliminated early on might sit and watch the contest unfold, tension rising as fewer and fewer were left in. One girl at my school was a beautiful runner, and I remember the thrill of watching her long legs eating up the track, sometimes passing the others twice.

Of course, some people have horrible memories of sports day, hating the feeling of being
15   last, or under pressure to win from families taking it too seriously. Too much success made others over-competitive – witness Jeffrey Archer bringing spiked running shoes along for the fathers' race at his children's school. But for most it was fun. One of the most abiding images of Princess Diana was of her running joyfully, shoes off and long neck extended, flying along the track in a mothers' event at her son's school, enjoying the simple pleasure
20   of the race.

But the sports day has changed.

25   Almost a third of schools no longer have them at all, arguing that children without a chance of winning get nothing out of them. One school has barred parents, claiming their presence upsets the children. Others have replaced what they see as old-fashioned competitive races with a new concept: the 'zone sport day'. It is increasingly popular, but like many compromises it is a poor, unhappy hodge-podge of a thing.

It does away with any individual competition and all obvious team competition, too. Children are sorted into ad hoc groups and go round a number of zones, doing a different activity at each one. For instance, they might run a relay but they will run it as a group, 30   non-competitively. Their time is recorded and then they go on to the next thing. At the very end, all of the times are added up and one group is declared to have won.

So instead of children running round a track, racing against each other while being cheered on by excited parents, they all shamble from zone to zone, not seeming to be particularly bothered about what's going on, or to be trying hard, or to be emotionally involved in any 35   way; in fact, many seem completely unaware of what is happening.

The scheme is supposed to have the advantage that all the children are active all of the time and therefore don't spend time watching each other, although cheering each other on and learning to appreciate the prowess of the natural athletes among them were surely some of the more inclusive aspects of the traditional sports day.

40   I can testify that, for the onlooker, the zone sports day is perhaps the most tedious kind of sporting contest ever devised. I would rather watch paint drying. Devising a race so that there is no risk of losing, and no thrill of winning, turns it into a dreary plod. More than tedious, it is depressing to watch the children doing something so pointless and boring. One wonders if it is a metaphor for the whole school experience, as they shuffle through 45   exercises devised by higher authorities, which no one has explained to them. They don't understand why it is being done this way and they haven't been given a choice.

Surely it is time to resurrect the sports day and to bring back competitive sport. It is good for children and they enjoy it. Competition focuses the mind. We need not encourage them to take it too seriously, and the 21st-century sports day is not going to recreate 50   19th-century social values, as some claim. The sack race, after all, will go the way of the sacks. But for heaven's sake, let's get some perspective. Running races is okay. The race may not always be to the swift (although it usually is), but for the rest of us the life skill we learned at sports day – of how to lose gracefully – is something that will never be out of date.

Passage 2

If you have any doubt about the intense and lasting psychological damage that can be wrought by competitive football, repeat after me: 'Scotland. World Cup. Argentina 1978.' In the pre-match sunshine of Buenos Aires, a reporter asked the Scottish manager, the late Ally McLeod, what he intended to do after the World Cup. 'Retain it,' answered the 5   ebullient McLeod, setting a benchmark for Scottish ineptitude that many have tried to equal but none has actually beaten. An entire generation's reserves of self-confidence were obliterated in one ill-starred adventure.

→

10 So, when a council's 'football development officers' insist that losing a match can have traumatic consequences, no Scot over the age of 25 is in a position to argue. Such mental scarring is bad enough for hardened football fans, who at least have alcohol and years of bitter experience to call upon. Just imagine what harm such trauma can wreak on young, impressionable minds.

15 Imagining is what we will soon have to do, however. Junior football teams in some parts of Scotland are to be banned from playing in league and cup competitions in order to protect them from the pain of losing. In future, the losing side (henceforth to be known as 'the runners-up') will be allowed to field two extra players. If one team is more than five goals ahead at half-time, the score will revert to nil–nil.

20 The rewriting of the Scottish rulebook echoes a row in England recently when an under-nine junior league match in Sheffield ended 29–0, a score duly reported in the local press. League officials have decreed that no scores above 14–0 can be made public and have asked the newspaper to refrain from publishing them. The fear is that playing for teams that suffer such heavy defeats humiliates children.

25 And they are right. But what the well-meaning officials fail to understand, however, is that learning how to lose is one of the most valuable lessons of childhood. The officials may believe that by eliminating the competitive element of football, they are concentrating on teaching skills and social interaction, but they are sending out a much more sinister message. Children will learn that the rules can be rewritten to suit yourself, that performance does not matter, that you need never push yourself to your absolute limit and that losing must be avoided at all costs. In short, they will learn that mediocrity is not 30 merely acceptable, it is desirable.

Most children are intensely competitive. They can turn anything into a contest: getting dressed, eating breakfast, breaking wind, behaving badly. You name it; it is much more fun if you pit yourself against a deadly rival, particularly if that happens to be a sibling. Attempting to eradicate competition from a child's life is as pointless and cruel as trying 35 to stifle their sense of humour.

Sport teaches children to work together in teams to achieve a common goal. It allows them to compete emotionally and physically in a controlled environment. It provides an acceptable outlet for feelings of aggression, and it teaches them how to harness negative emotions and turn them into something positive.

40 Any parent who has comforted a weeping child after a sporting disaster will sympathise with what the Council officials are trying to achieve. But they will also know that disappointment cannot be postponed indefinitely in life and that it is easier to bear the more often it happens. If you never experience the misery of losing, how can you experience the exhilaration of winning?

First: Identify very briefly the key point of similarity in the writers' attitudes to competitive sport for young people.

Next: Work through Passage 1 answering the questions below in note form.

1. Very briefly, describe the writer's feelings about 'school sports days' in:
   a) lines 1–7
   b) lines 8–13
   c) lines 14–20.

2. Re-read lines 22–26.
   a) Why, according to the writer, has the 'zone sport day' been introduced in a number of schools?
   b) What is the writer's attitude to the 'zone sport day'?
3. Re-read lines 27–46.
   a) What impression does the writer create in lines 32–35 of the 'zone sport day'?
   b) Explain the difference of opinion, in lines 36–39, between the writer and the advocates of the 'zone sport day'.
   c) What is the writer's main criticism in lines 40–46 of the 'zone sport day'?
4. What reasons does the writer give in the final paragraph (lines 47–54) in favour of the return of the traditional sports day?

Now: Work through Passage 2 answering the questions below in note form.

5. What key point is the writer making in lines 1–12?
6. What, according to the writer, are the changes she describes in lines 13–17 designed to achieve?
7. What point does the anecdote in lines 18–22 add to the writer's argument?
8. From lines 23–35, identify the key points the writer makes to justify her opinion that the 'well-meaning officials' (line 23) are wrong.
9. According to the writer in lines 36–44, what important benefits do children derive from sport?

Finally: Use your answers to the preceding questions to write a structured response to the following exam-type question.

> ### Question
>
> Both writers express their views about competitive sport for young people. Identify key areas on which they agree. In your answer, you should refer in detail to both passages.
>
> You may answer this question in continuous prose or in a series of developed bullet points.

SECTION 3 – EXAM PRACTICE

In this section you will find exam-length passages with an exam-style comparison question.

Here are some dos and don'ts to remember when you are attempting the Question on both Passages in the exam:

- **Do** check if you're being asked to deal with agreement or disagreement, or both, and do exactly as instructed. If, for example, the question asks about disagreement and you spot a couple of agreements, don't mention them.

- **Do** remember to stick to 'key areas' and don't include trivial ones. This is possibly the most difficult aspect of this question.

- **Do** try out early on in the year both ways of presenting your answer (formal continuous prose and developed bullet points), decide which one suits you best and then stick to that for all exams and tests.

- **Don't** assume you're being asked for **all** the agreements or disagreements you can see in the writers' points of view. There will always be a clear focus given to you, for example '… similarities in what the writers are saying about the benefits of legalising drugs …'

- **Don't** manufacture disagreements by saying that one writer mentions something that the other writer doesn't.

- **Don't** give any of your own views on the topic or on the writers' points of view – even if it's a topic you feel strongly about or even if you think one of the writers is talking nonsense. The task here is to provide an objective overview of what the writers are saying.

Answers

Answers for the exercises in this section can be found in the *Answers and Marking Schemes* book, on pages 20–23.

Exercise 7 – Teenagers

The following two passages focus on adults' attitudes to teenagers.

Read the passages and attempt the question that follows at the end of Passage 2. While reading, you may wish to make notes on the main ideas and/or highlight key points in the passage.

In the first passage Jenny McCartney, writing in *The Telegraph* newspaper, takes a fairly negative view of today's teenagers.

Passage 1

A miserable state of affairs has come to pass at St James's Church, near Rochdale. A malevolent gang of local teenagers has been intimidating elderly worshippers, forcing the Rev Robin Usher to hold weekday services in his home instead. The teenagers have taken to loafing around the church grounds and the graveyard, smoking dope and swigging alcopops. Sometimes they chuck stones and eggs at the church windows, or thunder up and down one wing of the church while the elderly folk cower in the other, struggling to keep their fraying thoughts on God.

The plight of the parishioners is by no means unusual: they are the hapless victims of The Rampaging Teenager, a burgeoning social phenomenon. Not so long ago The Teenager was a relatively benign figure, subject to jovial censure largely for sulkiness and a penchant for loud music. Now The Teenager is a national terror, filling older people with a queasy unease.

Every day The Teenager makes an unlovely appearance in the press, sometimes in the form of an individual who has perpetrated an especially shocking act, but more often as part of an uncontrollable mob, dissolving teachers' authority in jeering obscenities, terrorising bus drivers, wielding knives and mugging Tube passengers.

It is true, of course, that the thousands of exemplary adolescents hardly ever make the papers, apart from at exam results time when they are briefly emblazoned across the news pages, the gleam of their teeth competing with the high sheen of their results.

Yet even taking the press's preoccupation with wickedness into account, it seems indisputable that the minority of 'problem teenagers' – as once they would have been called – are becoming ever more violently problematic, just as adults are becoming ever more wary of confronting them. These two things are quite certainly connected.

When I am travelling on the top deck of the bus, for example, and gallumphing 15-year-olds are shrieking oaths, dropping litter, guzzling pungent kebabs and pushing one another about, do I stand up and demand that they sit down and behave like normal people? Of course I don't. I am worried that, by attempting any such gesture, I might be baited mercilessly until I can finally stumble off at my stop. I have little confidence that any other adult on the bus would back me up. Teenagers now are awful, I think.

But then, every so often, I have little flashbacks into my own unbalanced, excitable teenage psyche. I was reasonably respectful towards grown-ups, but – seen through adult eyes – my state of mind was far from normal. Several times a day, some minor idiosyncrasy I had observed in my teachers – people whom I broadly liked and respected – would trigger in me prolonged fits of helpless, tearful laughter. Almost everything seemed intensely funny, and few of us had any profound sense of consequence. I remember my English teacher, pale-faced, brandishing a large lead weight which he said had come hurtling down the stairwell, narrowly missing his head. The culprit was a quiet, quirky boy who had been rolling his interesting lead weight along the top of the stairwell when it tumbled off. It could have killed our teacher, but at the time we simply thought the incident a diverting little hoo-hah in a dull afternoon.

Yet such incidents were admittedly rare, and what contained their frequency – and prevented mere silliness from escalating into systematic taunting and aggression – was a sense of a unified adult authority, whereby parents, teachers, policemen and everyone else appeared to think as one, and were virtually certain to back each other up. That authority has been gradually eroded and fragmented by a tremulous, legalistic officialdom.

50 Teenagers do not quite understand, although they should, that a hurled egg might seem a great joke to them, but is a source of sheer terror to an elderly lady; but aside from a few very hard cases, they are more reckless than wicked. It is up to adults to assert their vanished authority over the lunatic adolescent fringe. That is why the congregation of St James's Church should spurn prayers in the vicarage next week, and – with a couple of towering policemen to hand – prepare to retake the church and its grounds.

In the second passage Kate Figgis, writing in *The Times* newspaper, takes a much more sympathetic view of teenagers.

Note

When the passage was written, there had been a suggestion that the voting age in the UK would be reduced to 16 'for the next election'. When this book was being prepared for publication (December 2014) 16 and 17-year-olds had been able to vote in the Independence Referendum and agreement had been reached that this would be the case for future elections to the Scottish Parliament. No such plans were in place for UK parliamentary elections.

Passage 2

Teenagers seem to make headlines only when it is bad news – binge-drinking, truancy, drug-taking, underage sex. No other age group is so consistently stereotyped, misunderstood or reviled. The public views them with suspicion – pedestrians will cross the street rather than pass three or four noisy teenagers on a street corner – while to
5 anyone working behind the counter, every teenager is a potential shoplifter. Meanwhile, parents complain endlessly about them: their untidy rooms, their selfishness, their back-chatting, the difficulty learning where they've been, what they've been doing and with whom.

So maybe it's unusual to say that I love teenagers. I love having my 15-year-old daughter's
10 friends in the house. I buy extra tubs of ice-cream just to keep them there, despite the extra clearing up. I love hearing them shriek happily. I love the way that six of them can cuddle up on a two-seater sofa discussing world poverty, eating popcorn in front of an episode of *Friends*.

Adolescents exist in a half world, often denied both the security of childhood and the
15 privileges and responsibilities of adulthood, with no obvious rites of passage, no clear path from one to the other. They're considered adult when it suits, but not when it doesn't; they have to pay adult prices and tax, but they still can't vote.

Last week it was revealed that the Government does, in fact, intend to give the vote to 16-year-olds after the next election – welcome news indeed, for it is high time that we
20 began to harness the passionate political energy of the young. Our political life feels so tired and short of ideas and solutions that it can only improve by involving them more.

We think of teenagers as materialistic, which they often are, yet this is also a time when they are at their most altruistic, idealistic and determined to make the world a better place. They begin to grasp the significance of more abstract concepts such as religion, relationships and mortality. They wake up to the wider world and feel outraged by its injustices. That anybody should be homeless when there are empty houses seems ludicrous. Wars are a crime against humanity – end of story.

Teenagers embrace concepts such as vegetarianism because of their need to do something when they feel angry about animal welfare. They can argue for hours about political ideas and be caring and public-spirited provided they are given opportunities and encouraged to do so. Their arguments are often simplistic and categoric, for they have yet to develop a deeper understanding of how hard it is to find solutions to the world's major problems. But their idealism is fresh and forthright, passionate to the point where it can challenge the old fogeys.

We criticise adolescents for being rebellious and rejecting authority, but maybe they are just being honest, an attribute that we lose the moment we need to please a boss. Teenagers have the energy and the daring to challenge bureaucracy and pointless rules. 'You can't wear two pairs of earrings at school but you can wear one. But if you can wear one, why not two?'

Teenagers may be morose and monosyllabic at times, but they can also be hilarious. They love to exercise their expanding intellectual skills playing with irony and puns. And where would we be without the vibrancy of youth culture, without the pop anthems? Our language is kept alive with new definitions of words such as 'cool', 'fit' or 'safe'.

Teenagers are acutely sensitive and vulnerable. They often mask a deep sense of self-doubt with bravado. Negative images of teenagers do not do them any favours, for such stereotypes reinforce negative images about themselves when they feel down. If we tell them that they are selfish, lazy good-for-nothings, they just rise to those expectations: we create the impression that that is how you have to behave to be a teenager today.

But if we look for the positive we find in the young a well full of potential. Teenagers may seem like threatening outsiders, but that is because we fail as a society to integrate them as valuable constituents. They will behave in a more mature manner only when they are afforded respect and more adult responsibilities. Giving 16-year-olds the vote is one significant step, for it tells them that their views matter and includes them in a political process from which many feel alienated.

Question

Both writers express their views about teenagers. Identify key areas on which they disagree. In your answer, you should refer in detail to both passages.

You may answer this question in continuous prose or in a series of developed bullet points.

Exercise 8 – The importance of reading

The following passages were both written by well-known writers of children's fiction.

The first is by Michael Morpurgo (author of more than 50 books, including *War Horse*, *Why the Whales Came* and *Kensuke's Kingdom*) and was printed in *The Times* newspaper.

The second is by Anthony Horowitz, author of the 'Alex Rider, teenage spy' books, and is part of a public lecture that was subsequently printed in *The Telegraph* newspaper.

The two passages focus on the importance of reading – especially by children.

Read the passages and attempt the question that follows at the end of Passage 2. While reading, you may wish to make notes on the main ideas and/or highlight key points in the passage.

Passage 1

[…] For the past 18 months in my role as Children's Laureate I have been travelling the country telling stories to young readers and young writers, telling how this particular weaver of tales writes his stories. Like some superannuated strolling player, I have set up and performed wherever anyone would let me: in tiny village halls, grand concert halls, in
5 tents and bookshops and school halls and, once, in an old people's home; from audiences of 14 children in the small island school on Jura in the Hebrides, to 2500 people in the Albert Hall. […]

[…] Hundreds of my fellow writers, and storytellers, illustrators, librarians, teachers and booksellers, are doing just what I've been doing. […] This kind of sustained effort to bring
10 children to books and books to children is much needed and is, in my view, the most effective way of persuading children to become readers and writers.

[…] Here is someone in front of them who loves stories, who tells them with such passion that the world of reading, the sheer joy, fun and wonder of it, can be opened up to children who may never have enjoyed books at all. A young life can be changed that way, enriched for ever.

15 […] So why do we fail to engage so many children? Why do millions of them never become readers? After all this commitment, why is there this divide in our society: books beloved by some and ignored and regarded as irrelevant by others? Why are stories not central to our culture, unless they are on television? Why do so many feel alienated from their literary heritage? The convenient answer is the usual answer. Blame someone.
20 Parents, teachers, librarians, publishers, bookshops, the media or the Government. The uncomfortable truth, I have concluded, after years as a father, teacher, writer and, now, as strolling player, is that we are all responsible because we are not being honest about this. Parents who do not read to their children enough at night, teachers who use books simply as educational tools for the literacy hour, librarians who allow their libraries
25 to become drab, publishers who publish too much rubbish (there are 10,000 children's titles published a year) and writers – for we are complicit in this overproduction – are all responsible.

[…] The question […] should not be 'Who is to blame?' but 'What can be done about it?'. What practical steps can be taken to make reading and writing more inclusive
30 and attractive for our children? If we want our children to be literate, to love stories, then bring storytelling back into the mainstream media. We had *Listen with Mother*, […] we had *Jackanory*. Where are they now? Radio and television can help hugely here. Bring parents in on the act. […] That is how reading should begin, almost with the mother's milk, that intimate story between parent and child. Because […]

35 we know it will often be through the teacher that a child first hears a story. Many great teachers find the time to read stories and to read them well, so that children will hear the music in the words, and will laugh and cry with the teacher.

[…] Thus enriched, the teacher can pass on his or her own love of stories to the children, can talk of books and writing and reading with confidence, fervour and delight. Teach the
40 children a love of story, of the music of words first, give them the delight, inspire them to write themselves, then the need for literacy begins to make sense – literature before literacy, then.

How can this be done? Unchain the teachers, take the fear of targets away, unlock their creative potential, give them back their freedom to teach what it is they love. Trust them.
45 Let there be half an hour at the end of school simply for telling and reading stories, a wonderful wind-down at the end of each day. But don't ask questions afterwards, just let the children listen and enjoy, and lose themselves in the magic of it.

[…] We need […] to exercise our children's imaginative powers through reading and writing. For what is education if not to broaden our horizons, give us knowledge, understanding
50 and insight and the opportunity to empathise and learn about ourselves and the complex world around us? I know no better way for a child, or a grown-up child, to do this than through books.

Passage 2

Children and reading seems to be a hot topic. Do boys read? Are they reading less than girls? These are questions that are being asked more and more often – and recently the Government climbed on the bandwagon. But who cares? Does it really matter who's reading what – and, at a time when increasing numbers of children's books are being launched
5 with ever larger fanfares, what is it that we are all chasing? Culture, literacy, civilisation and enlightenment? Or film deals and six-figure advances?

The Government has announced a £27 million initiative to distribute 9 million books to children up to the age of four. 'Every child deserves the best start in life,' it proclaims. 'And there is no better time to get parents into the habit of reading with their children than
10 when they are little.' It is embracing the work of Booktrust, an independent educational charity founded in the 19th century, which has, indeed, managed to place millions of books into the hands of infants and children.

I admire the work of Booktrust, but I was surprised that nobody showed the least concern about this new alliance. Because it seems to me that, at a stroke, the agenda has changed.
15 We have moved from pure altruism – the sharing of an enthusiasm – to the simplistic attitude of another governmental tick list. Reading is good for you. The Government is giving kids books. So the Government is good for you.

Consider the dangers. If politicians and their advisers become involved in this project, who will end up choosing the books? And how long will it be before certain rules – of political
20 correctness and good citizenship – set in? Once the Government is involved, what will happen to publishers who entertain writers like me? Would my own publisher be happy for me to be critical of the Government if, at the same time, it was negotiating a contract for several million copies of *Maisie Mouse*? Perhaps I'm being paranoid but I think we should be wary of lines getting crossed.

→

25 What I most dislike about the Government's take on literacy is this 'nanny state' feeling that reading is good for you. I just hate the idea that if you read, you're going to be all right; that books can act like vitamins or diet supplements to make a healthier, happier human being.

I love books. I love reading. I can't imagine my life without it. But I do resent the idea of
30 reading being some sort of virtue, a sort of gold medal that you can pin on the lapel of some pink-faced, grinning child. I hate parents who tell me that their little Gemma is only nine but already she's halfway through *War and Peace*. It all seems so Victorian – and it's hypocritical, too.

Are adults reading? And what are they reading? And how bad does a book have to be
35 before it's not worth reading at all? Step forward Jeffrey Archer, perhaps. Does reading *Hello!* magazine count as reading? How about Mills & Boon? Where do you draw the line between literature and (not to put too fine a point on it) crap? When does reading become good for you?

People like Dan Brown's books, although I think his writing is terrible, with its clichés, its
40 melodramatic bombast and its clumsy constructions. Well, it's easy enough to sneer at Dan Brown, but however critical you want to be, you have to admit that his stories – and in particular, of course, *The Da Vinci Code* – are wonderfully readable. That's what's made him even richer than J.K. Rowling. His books sell in millions. Whether they have any inherent value is actually irrelevant. And that is precisely my point. Reading is enjoyable. I can't
45 imagine my life without books. All my work has been informed by my love of Dickens, Hardy, Austen, Orwell and so on. I like Stephen King, too. And Ian Fleming.

But reading is not necessarily a quick fix, and we delude ourselves if we think that it is. The boy who reads is not necessarily better than the boy who doesn't. Did Beethoven read? Did Mozart? Does Bill Gates, or Richard Branson? I sometimes think we're trying to turn
50 reading into a universal panacea. It's many things – but it certainly isn't that.

Question

Both writers express their views about the importance of reading among children. Identify key areas on which they agree and on which they disagree. In your answer, you should refer in detail to both passages.

You may answer this question in continuous prose or in a series of developed bullet points.

Exercise 9 – Sex education

The following two passages focus on the topic of sex education in schools.

Read the passages and attempt the question that follows at the end of Passage 2. While reading, you may wish to make notes on the main ideas and/or highlight key points in the passage.

In the first passage Joyce McMillan, writing in *The Scotsman* newspaper, discusses reaction to a suggestion that five-year-olds should be given sex education and reflects on how our society responds to change.

Passage 1

For the last 30 years or so, British society has found itself in a kind of limbo, unable to move backwards, yet somehow reluctant to move on. In our hearts and minds, we seem to be resisting the changes with which we live from day to day, as if every statistic recording numbers of children born out of wedlock, or numbers of migrants arriving in Britain, or
5   numbers of teenagers enjoying an active sex life, represents a deep threat to our world, and therefore to ourselves.

So it could have been almost anything that triggered the latest round of shock-horror headlines about a nation going to hell in a handcart, but, as it was, it was a public comment by an eminent doctor, advocating that children as young as five should be receiving sex
10   education in schools. His reasoning is simple: children, he argues, need a good, confident knowledge of the facts about sex, long before they are even tempted to start experimenting themselves.

There was no chance, though, of his remarks being greeted with calm agreement all round. For this is a culture where, well within living memory, children as old as 13 or 14 were
15   forbidden to know anything about sex at all, sometimes with tragic consequences. Put the words 'five-year-olds' and 'sex education' together, therefore, and the old atavistic monster rears up, roaring phrases like 'going to the dogs' or 'pouring petrol on a fire'.

Now, of course, it's possible to debate at length whether or not, under current conditions, the extension of sex education in schools would make any decisive impact on that group
20   of vulnerable British youngsters who, for a blizzard of social reasons, just can't seem to associate what they are told about sex at school with what happens in their own lives. It seems to me, though, that it's not really the substance of the issue that's in question here. In reason, we all know that five-year-olds need to know a little bit about sex, even if it's only why their own bodies are as they are. It's just that we don't like seeing that truth
25   written down in so many words, and we don't like the idea that we can't rely on families alone to do the job.

And the mood is the same in dozens of areas where our society should be moving forward to deal with the practical challenges of 21st-century life, but, at some deeper level, seems to have come to the limit of its capacity for change.

30   So what are we to do, stranded in this no-man's-land between an old civilisation that's no longer sustainable either practically or morally, and a new one that we still resist because it seems somehow alien? Some bluster hopelessly about the need to return to the past. Others talk blithely as if there was no problem about abandoning the family as a useful transmitter of wisdom, and passing the whole job on to schools.

→

35 But for the rest of us – well, we probably do best when we face the truth that all social change involves some measure of loss, but that the clock cannot be turned back towards attitudes and prejudices that were abandoned for the best of reasons. And, above all, we perhaps need to strive to move forward as a whole society, rather than as a bunch of fragmented individuals demanding increasingly impossible feats from our hard-pressed
40 public services.

For in the end, schools can teach nothing that society as a whole does not want children to learn. If our society eats junk food, schools cannot make children eat healthily. If our society is full of bullying behaviour, schools catch the backwash of emotional and physical violence. And if our society remains hopelessly ambivalent about sex – so recently an
45 unspoken taboo, now a multimedia nightmare of cheap raunch and smut – well, then it's not primarily the failure of teachers that leaves so many teenagers all at sea in this key area of their lives. It's rather our own embarrassment and silence, passed on from generation to generation, and whether lessons begin at five or 15, it will take more than a change in education policy to make any difference to that.

In the second passage below, Minette Marrin, writing in *The Times* newspaper, discusses Government proposals to increase the amount of sex education in schools.

Passage 2

According to the old saying, those who can, do, and those who can't, teach. I have come to think that those who can't teach, teach sex education.

Judged by its results – not a bad way of judging – sex education has been an utter failure. The increase in sex education here in recent years has coincided with an explosion of
5 unwanted pregnancies and sexually transmitted disease (STD) far worse than anywhere else in Europe. Since the Government's teenage pregnancy strategy was introduced, the number of girls having abortions has soared. A culture of promiscuity among the young has driven the rate of STDs to a record. Almost 400,000 – half of them under 25 – were newly diagnosed in the past year, 6% more than two years ago. You might well be tempted
10 to argue that sex education causes sexual delinquency.

When something fails, the usual procedure is to drop it and try something else. With sex education, however, the worse it gets, the more people cry out for more of it and earlier – to the extent that Ministers are considering making schools offer more sex education, offer it earlier and deny parents the right to withdraw their children from it.

15 Last week the Family Planning Association – now calling itself the fpa, having joined other charities in a mad rush to reduce themselves to a couple of lower-case letters – published a comic-style sex education booklet ('Let's Grow with Nisha and Joe') for six-year-olds, to be marketed in primary schools for use in sex and relationships lessons. There's nothing wrong with the pamphlet itself. Admittedly it's more of a dreary workbook
20 than a 'fun' comic, but there's nothing that would startle a child or should upset even the most conservative of 'family campaigners'. The rudest thing is a drawing of two children, naked, with instructions to draw lines connecting interesting bits of their bodies with the appropriate words, yet it seems to me highly unrealistic (given that 25% of children leave primary school struggling to read and write) to assume that many six-year-olds could
25 begin to read the labels 'testicles' or 'vagina'.

What I really object to about the book is what I object to about sex education as a whole. Sex education – particularly compulsory and standardised sex education – is based on mistaken assumptions. The first is the pervasive assumption of equality – that is, that all six-year-olds or all 11-year-olds or 15-year-olds can discuss the complexities of sex in the

30 same form in the same way. That's nonsense. Children vary in intelligence and in progress. Children and teenagers mature at different ages and come from different backgrounds. You cannot talk the same way to a shy 13-year-old who hasn't had her first period as to another who is well acquainted with the darker recesses of the school bike shed. Some boys are men at 11 and 12, physically; others are children until much later. You cannot talk

35 to all these children together. And it undermines the authority of those parents who do not share the values of the teacher.

Another mistaken assumption is that sex education ought, necessarily, to be entrusted to teachers, given how wildly they vary in ability and in moral attitudes. The thought that the Government is considering making sex and relationship education compulsory in

40 schools is terrifying. I can hardly imagine anything worse than subjecting a sensitive child to guidance on such matters from an inexperienced and politically correct teacher, who is neither well informed nor self-critical. The relationships between sex, love, babies and disease are too explosive to be left primarily to such a person, or to any person apart from the parents.

Question

Both writers express their views about sex education in schools. Identify key areas on which they agree and on which they disagree. In your answer, you should refer in detail to both passages.

You may answer this question in continuous prose or in a series of developed bullet points.

PART FOUR

RUAE PRACTICE PAPERS

In this part of the book, there are six full-length practice exercises in Reading for Understanding, Analysis and Evaluation. Their style is based on the Specimen Question Paper for Higher English published in February 2014.

It is difficult to gauge the comparative difficulty of these six exercises, but the choice of order has been predicated on the idea that the first two are on subjects fairly familiar to young adults that therefore might provide a comfortable starting point. No attempt has been made, however, to provide 'transition' exercises between the level of demand at National 5 and Higher: these are all full-blown Higher exercises.

There is a minimum level of competence to be reached before any benefit can be gained from tackling the practice papers. The work in Part One of this book is designed to help with building the necessary knowledge and skills to tackle the questions on the first passage; the work in Part Three will have prepared students for the question on both passages.

These exercises can be used for early diagnostic assessment but their best potential is probably to be realised in the second half of the course, when the students are sufficiently skilled so as to make a meaningful attempt at tackling a full-scale exam exercise.

Answers

Answers for the exercises in this part can be found in the *Answers and Marking Schemes* book, on pages 24–54.

PAPER 1 – HOMEWORK

The following two passages focus on homework.

In the first passage Richard Morrison, writing in *The Times* newspaper, questions the value of homework, after a leading school announced it was going to reduce the amount of homework its pupils had to do.

Passage 1

Some poems strike a chord. Others ring a bell. But Philip Larkin's 'Toads' bongs like Big Ben inside my head. In the poem he says work is a like a toad and asks 'Why should I let the toad work squat on my life?'

5   The toad work has certainly squatted on my life. It has controlled, constrained and coloured (or discoloured) it. There aren't many waking hours when I'm not thinking about it. And of the 12,000-odd days that I've notched up as a theoretically free-willed adult, far too few have passed without me bowing to it. Unlike Larkin, however, I don't think that it is fear – of losing my pension, upsetting the boss, or whatever – that keeps me in this work-addicted state. It's guilt. And I know exactly where and when that guilt originated. At
10 school, 40 years ago.

The school was, and is, a fine institution. But as with most aspirational schools, competing fiercely for status and places at 'top' universities, it tended to instil a feeling that nothing could be achieved in life without hard slog – hours and hours of it, after school, every evening. At 14 I was doing two hours of homework a night; by 17 it was more like five.
15 Consequently my exam results were sparkling. But my social life was the opposite. Even at parties, the memory of quadratic equations still to be solved and irregular French verbs left unconjugated hung over me like a cloud. As for any interest in the world outside, how could I develop that? There weren't enough hours in the day.

What's worse, the nagging sense of guilt if I wasn't working persisted through university
20 and into my adult life. It lingers even now, this feeling that time not spent doing the job is time wasted.

Homework has a lot to answer for. It doesn't mess up every child. But the mental oppression of leaving school for the day, and then facing hours of slog, alienates many. And there's another sizeable minority in whom it triggers a cosmic conscientiousness, out of all
25 proportion to the task at hand, that will blight the rest of their lives, impinging not just on social activities but on their responsibilities as parents too. This is tragic, because those are the very people whose work ethic and intellectual capability could be so vital for society, if properly balanced by a healthy attitude to recreation and family life.

→

30 In the 40 years since I last wore a blazer, the culture of excessive homework, especially in 'high-flying' schools, has become far worse. There is one obvious reason for that. Education is now controlled by a generation of politicians who, on the whole, have no cultural hinterlands themselves – no interests outside politics. So they find it almost impossible to understand the value of giving children the time and opportunities to discover the infinite richness and possibilities of life. The narrowing of the educational curriculum in
35 this country over the past 30 years – pushing art, music, sport and drama to the margins or beyond – has been shocking.

At the same time the fetish with league tables has forced teachers to turn schools into fact-cramming, rote-learning factories in which narrowly focused lessons are reinforced by stacks of homework. Our education system is now as blinkered, as grindingly utilitarian,
40 as in the era mocked by Dickens in *Hard Times*. Is it any wonder that so many school-leavers have no pastimes except shopping, watching telly and binge-drinking?

So the news that a leading state school has announced a huge reduction in its homework requirements, releasing five or more hours each week for a broader exploration of the world, brought joy to my heart. Especially as the initiative seems to be part of a wider move among
45 free-thinking schools to recognise – or rather, to recognise again, after decades of denial – the importance of non-curricular activities in the nurturing of a rounded individual.

The question is whether this trend can be turned into a sea-change. Don't underestimate the difficulties of doing that. Thousands of playing fields have been sold. There are far fewer after-school groups, such as Scouts or youth clubs, around. Lots of parents are only
50 too grateful if their kids get sacks of homework, because then they don't feel any obligation to devise activities themselves to stimulate their offspring's minds. And teachers have become so conditioned to following a narrow curriculum to the letter that many would feel terrified if asked to run 'enrichment activities'.

But change the system we must. Piling mountains of homework on children is the surest
55 way to turn education into drudgery. And once that happens, curiosity dies and a soulless, sullen, mechanistic compliance takes over. The lucky ones escape the system as soon as they can and start exploring the world properly. The unlucky ones never escape. Larkin's toad has got them in his clutches for life.

I know. I'm still there.

In the second passage, Eleanor Mills, writing in *The Sunday Times* newspaper in October 2012, comments on an announcement by the President of France that he planned to abolish homework in France.

Passage 2

It is every working parent's nightmare. You stagger through the door, knackered, longing for a drink – or just a chance to stare at the wall for a few minutes – and instead find yourself supervising what seems an unremitting flow of homework. While I loathe it, I also believe the whole rigmarole is essential. Last week the President of France announced
5 that he wanted to abolish homework, his argument being that homework increases social inequality because wealthier children are more likely than their poorer peers to have parents who will help them do it. In this, as in so much else, he is wrong.

I am in favour of homework because I believe it consolidates in a child's mind what they have been taught at school and, more importantly, reinforces that holy grail of character
10 development: delayed gratification.

The value of homework is in the transaction around it, the age-old bargain of: do your homework and then you can watch television/go out and kick a football/play on the computer. My grandmother had a maxim that was drummed into me: business before pleasure. Accepting deferred gratification is one of the life skills parents must teach their
15 children, and homework plays a key role in nurturing the ability to delay instant pleasure in return for a bigger long-term reward. Setting up a culture in the home that effort will be rewarded has huge long-term benefits. If you make your offspring do their homework and then reward them, you are setting them up with a valuable blueprint for life.

Homework, of course, is not just about developing character; it also works on an academic
20 level – homework, particularly in secondary schools, has been shown by numerous research projects to improve educational attainment, particularly when it is done with a motivated and engaged adult. That is not shorthand for 'middle class': many immigrant groups who do well educationally (Chinese, Indians and Nigerians in particular) have below-average incomes but motivated and engaged parents who set great store by learning. When such
25 a parent helps a child with their homework, they transmit those values. For children from chaotic families, school homework clubs can serve a similar role: pupils stay behind after school to complete their homework with help from teachers. This helps them overcome the lack of support at home.

Being pro-homework is not a popular stance, however. The President's plans have been
30 greeted with gleeful joy by all manner of pontificators, some of whom have been waging an anti-homework crusade for years, and in the past few days the media have been awash with lazy parents falling over themselves to agree with the French President.

Of course, I don't endorse the phenomenon of hyper-parenting or the kind of tiger mothering on display in a recent television documentary that showed pre-school
35 children being forced to do hours of homework every night, their heads drooping on to their books with exhaustion. Such relentless drilling of little ones risks putting them off learning for life.

From the age of seven or so, however, when children have to start learning their tables and mastering spelling, half an hour of homework to reinforce that day's lesson or practising
40 for a test, or reading aloud, has to be beneficial.

Many parents complain that homework has become a battleground, souring the precious time in the evenings they have as a family. But being a parent isn't about being your child's best mate; it's about making sure they have the tools to succeed in life. Learning to buckle down and get on with it, even if it's the last thing you feel like, is the cornerstone
45 of success.

Questions

Passage 1 Questions

1. By referring to lines 1–10, explain in your own words why the writer agrees so strongly with the poem 'Toads'.   3

2. Re-read lines 11–21.
   a) Identify **two** key problems the writer suffered as a result of working hard at school.   2
   b) By referring to at least two features of language in these lines, analyse how the writer's use of language conveys the unpleasantness he associates with schoolwork. In your answer you should refer to features such as word choice, sentence structure, imagery …   4

3. Identify **four** negative effects of homework the writer gives in lines 22–36.   4

4. The writer's tone when he is describing the effects of school league tables in lines 37–41 is one of contempt. By referring closely to these lines, analyse how his use of language creates this tone. In your answer you should refer to such features as word choice, imagery, sentence structure …   4

5. Re-read lines 42–53.
   Explain what advantages the writer thinks would come from a reduction in homework, but why it might be difficult to achieve.   4

6. Evaluate the effectiveness of the last two paragraphs (lines 54–59) as a conclusion to the passage as a whole. You should refer in your answer to ideas and language.   4

Passage 2 Question

7. Both writers express their views about homework. Identify key areas on which they disagree. In your answer, you should refer in detail to both passages.

   You may answer this question in continuous prose or in a series of developed bullet points.   5

PAPER 2 – *BREAKING BAD*

The following two passages focus on the American TV series *Breaking Bad*.

> ## Note
> No knowledge of the programme is needed to understand the passages or to answer the questions.

In the first passage Neil Mackay, writing in *The Sunday Herald* newspaper in October 2013, discusses the status of *Breaking Bad* as art.

Passage 1

In our multi-channel world of endless choice, many readers might not have seen *Breaking Bad*, but they will certainly have heard of it. Here's a brief catch-up: it started five years ago with an ordinary, dull, middle-aged high-school chemistry teacher, Walter White, who discovers that he has terminal cancer and turns to the illegal manufacture
5   of 'crystal meth' in order to make enough money to provide comfortably for his family after his death. Come last Monday, and five seasons in, Walter White had descended to sulphurous depths of evil, his family and everyone who came within his orbit destroyed by his ambition, pride and ruthlessness.

The show ended in a crescendo of fan hysteria, media hype, five-star critical adoration, and
10   ratings studio chiefs would open a vein for. Its finale was a seminal moment for television and a masterclass in what TV can do as an art form. This is a type of television that is trying to be almost Dickensian. In fact, forget trying – it is Dickensian. This is writing that takes powerful, believable characters, places them in a contemporary, realistic setting and allows their lives to play out over a long period of time in order to deconstruct our society
15   and entertain and excite the viewer.

Dickens was the master of the long-form novel – he drip-fed his stories out in the pages of Victorian magazines, hooked his public, had the straightforward punters hanging on his every word and the arty critics standing on their hind legs to applaud. And, of course, once Dickens had told his story in the pages of magazines such as *Household Words*, he then
20   brought out the complete novel – often in time for Christmas. (The complete box set of *Breaking Bad* is in the shops at the end of November.)

→

25 The literary comparisons, though, get even loftier. What started as a darkly comic crime show deepened into a drama commonly referred to as Shakespearean, with White often compared to Macbeth. The Shakespearean analogy is only a little overblown – because in terms of what Western culture is producing at the moment *Breaking Bad* is among the very best. The novel may still be the high point of that culture, but a show like *Breaking Bad* comes thrillingly close to challenging its supremacy. If even 20 per cent of television was like *Breaking Bad* then the novel might have to step into second place among the art forms that best express and analyse the spirit of the age.

30 *Breaking Bad* is the pinnacle of a decade-long march by US programme makers that threatens to elevate television to real art, not just in terms of storytelling, but in its capacity to fulfil art's most fundamental role: to eviscerate the society from which it emanated. It began with *The Sopranos*. Then came *The Wire*, *Mad Men* and a slew of other long-form TV serials that left nearly everyone looking hopelessly amateur in their wake.

35 *Breaking Bad* isn't just a spur-of-the moment fad that bloomed this summer and will be forgotten about in a month or two. Great art lives on because people talk about it, because it becomes embedded in culture and because people interpret it in many different ways as they start to co-opt it to fit their own worldview. There are bloggers in Beijing today dissecting the show and musing that it proves the degeneracy of America. Walter White
40 breaks bad because he reckons he is poor, and he is not just rejecting his fate, but also rejecting the evils of the capitalist system.

Meanwhile, over in the States, a writer uses *Breaking Bad* to support her fundamentalist Christian agenda. The show, while morally ambivalent throughout – often putting the viewer in the position of emotionally supporting the most villainous characters – did end
45 with what some critics saw as a rather black-and-white morality, with evil punished, good rewarded and those in need of redemption redeemed.

However, as with all good art, I suspect the audience hasn't yet realised how subversive and dangerous it is. It says something very dark about American capitalism: it says it will eat you up and spit you out; it will destroy you; it will make you a monster. It also says
50 something horrible and powerful about the state of modern masculinity. Walter is on the ultimate male power trip: his fragile, dangerous male sense of self has been beaten down by what he sees as humiliations of enormous proportions – being a failure in the bedroom, being poorer than some of his students – and he will do anything to even the score against a world that he believes wronged him at every turn.

55 Walter White is truly a tragic character – because he is his own nemesis and the agent of his own ruin – and like all tragic characters he is also a fool. He may be smart, but he doesn't see the truth about himself until it is too late.

In the second passage, Jenny McCartney, writing in *The Telegraph* newspaper in August 2013, discusses her reaction to the programme.

Passage 2

For some time now, the British viewing public has essentially been divided into those who have and those who haven't yet seen the US television show *Breaking Bad*. The people who haven't seen it may be dimly aware that it is an enormously successful series in America. The people who have seen it have quite often become obsessed.

5   I stumbled on *Breaking Bad* by accident one night and pretty soon I was hooked too. As you travel through the series, the sense of danger sporadically thickens, tightens and relaxes again, but the inexorable direction is towards the heart of darkness. The creator of the show, Vince Gilligan, describes Walter White's dramatic trajectory as 'from Mr Chips to Scarface'.

10   Yet since the first eight episodes of series five finished, fans have been suspended in a state of high anticipation, awaiting the eight final episodes to come. The burning question of how the saga of Walter White's expanding drug empire will end has been tormenting aficionados. He's now definitely getting very close to Scarface, or perhaps something even harder and darker, more precisely focused in his ruthlessness. Unlike the cocaine-addled

15   Scarface, Walter doesn't sample his own merchandise: his high comes from winning the criminal game.

We've had box-set fever before, of course, with series such as *The Sopranos*, *The Wire* and *Mad Men*, but *Breaking Bad* has triggered perhaps its most extreme outbreak yet. Like *The Sopranos* the show features a protagonist who is also an antagonist, but while Tony Soprano

20   was someone born and raised in darkness, Walter White deliberately abandons the light for the darkness.

The critical acclaim for *Breaking Bad* also represents the most recent triumph for the medium of television. As recently as 15 years ago, television was routinely considered the poor cousin of film. Cinema, it was thought, boasted the panoramic vision, the auteurs

25   and proper actors, the big ideas, the philosophical depth: television churned out soapy schlock for loyal couch potatoes. Cinema, of course, still retains its power to move and mesmerise. Yet in recent years the studios have too often seemed to believe that success lies in bludgeoning audiences into awed submission with spectacle, rather than enticing them with close developments in character and plot.

30   Is *Breaking Bad* the best television series I have seen? Yes, if by 'best' one means possessing a narrative strong enough to nail viewers to their seats, while making us care about characters we might once only have despised. Spectacle is when we gawp at a tower block collapsing, and reach for more popcorn. Drama is when we are rendered breathless by the fear of what might happen to a specific individual in a single room on the 12th floor. One

35   of the rules of *Breaking Bad* is that the drama is always in the driving seat: in this case, the drama of how badness can creep into a man's character – bit by bit, choice by choice – until it has slowly consumed him from the inside, leaving only a hollow where the soul should be. Finally, it peeps out through his eyes. For all his intelligence, Walter seems oblivious to the takeover – but we can see it.

40   Walter is a wolf in suburban lamb's clothing. He seethes with paradoxes: he lowers himself into the toxic criminal underworld with an apparent purity of motive – the desire to provide financially after his death for his pregnant wife and their teenage son with cerebral palsy – yet the nature of his business places his family in enormous danger from Mexican cartels and their US-based representatives.

45 He displays, at times, extraordinary diligence and courage in the service of a corrupt and corrupting enterprise: all his positive qualities flow into a vast negative. Walter's vigorous efforts to dominate the crystal-meth business are like a dark parody of the American dream of enterprise and reward. The closeness of death, in some ways, has freed him from the dull constraints of good behaviour: he has less to lose.

50 *Breaking Bad* is certainly a violent series, unfurling as it does in a world wherein violence is the ultimate means of economic conversation. It is also a highly moral one: throughout the series, in a string of differing, extreme situations, each character reveals – sometimes surprisingly – the relative elasticity of their ethical code. Actions are taken, and rebound upon their perpetrator; killings exact their toll on both the victim and the murderer;
55 no death is free of consequences. *Breaking Bad* is a series that eschews didacticism but remembers that moral arguments are the most exciting ones audiences can have.

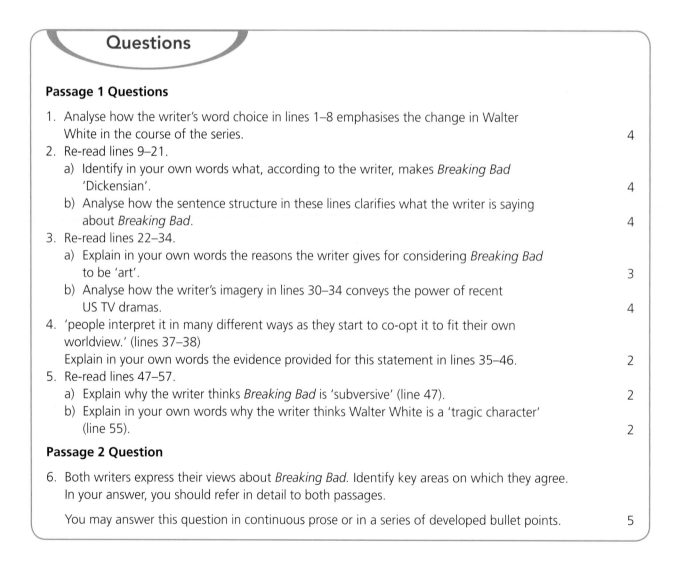

Questions

Passage 1 Questions

1. Analyse how the writer's word choice in lines 1–8 emphasises the change in Walter White in the course of the series.   4
2. Re-read lines 9–21.
   a) Identify in your own words what, according to the writer, makes *Breaking Bad* 'Dickensian'.   4
   b) Analyse how the sentence structure in these lines clarifies what the writer is saying about *Breaking Bad*.   4
3. Re-read lines 22–34.
   a) Explain in your own words the reasons the writer gives for considering *Breaking Bad* to be 'art'.   3
   b) Analyse how the writer's imagery in lines 30–34 conveys the power of recent US TV dramas.   4
4. 'people interpret it in many different ways as they start to co-opt it to fit their own worldview.' (lines 37–38)
   Explain in your own words the evidence provided for this statement in lines 35–46.   2
5. Re-read lines 47–57.
   a) Explain why the writer thinks *Breaking Bad* is 'subversive' (line 47).   2
   b) Explain in your own words why the writer thinks Walter White is a 'tragic character' (line 55).   2

Passage 2 Question

6. Both writers express their views about *Breaking Bad*. Identify key areas on which they agree. In your answer, you should refer in detail to both passages.

   You may answer this question in continuous prose or in a series of developed bullet points.   5

PAPER 3 – CONSERVATION

The following two passages focus on aspects of conservation.

In the first passage Magnus Linklater, writing in *The Times* newspaper in December 2008, discusses a plan to reintroduce beavers into the Scottish Highlands.

Passage 1

There are times when the world of nature conservation lurches dangerously close to lunacy. Its real purpose should be to conserve our natural heritage. All too often, however, it finds itself inventing a heritage all of its own, forgetting the basic laws of natural history.

5 Some time next year, a colony of 17 beavers, imported from Norway, will be released in the Scottish Highlands, part of a pilot project to see whether they can be introduced more widely. The hope is that these nose-twitching, undoubtedly endearing creatures will become a familiar part of the Scottish countryside.

It is far from clear why this is being done. Scottish National Heritage (SNH), which is behind the project, argues that beavers were once common in Britain, and that it would
10 be nice to have them back. It quotes European legislation in its support, saying that the EU Habitats Directive requires member states to reintroduce extinct species. 'The beaver is a charismatic species that would serve to raise wider biodiversity issues such as riparian woodland management, aspen restoration, wetland biodiversity and dead wood habitat,' says its website. The very language seems obscure, let alone the intent behind it.

15 Closer study of the beaver reveals that, while it may once have been familiar, it has been extinct in Britain for a very long time. The last records of it being found here date back to the 16th century. It appears to have been driven out as farming land extended and trees were cleared. Quite possibly, the managers of salmon rivers and lochs found its habit of gnawing through trees, building dams and burrowing into river banks a threat to local economies.
20 Conservation bodies did not exist in those days, so the beaver's fate was sealed.

I can understand the arguments for reintroducing a species that has only recently become extinct – the osprey, wiped out in the early part of the 20th century, is a good example. But taking this huge ecological leap back to the Middle Ages seems perverse, if not mildly insane. Then, Britain was clothed in forests, with wolves, bears and other wild animals
25 roaming the land. Today we have a land cleared for agriculture.

SNH, however, argues that beavers can have 'a positive impact upon local wildlife and can become significant wildlife tourism attractions for local economies'. It says that 73 per cent of the people of mid-Argyll support the idea, and that the project will be closely monitored. Quite who constitutes this 73 per cent is unclear. No local farmer, angler, landowner or
30 river manager, as far as I know, has ever supported the project. Anyone involved in the one industry that makes money in the Highlands – fishing – views the imminent arrival of the beavers with horror. Robin Malcolm, who farms 1000 acres in Knapdale, said he was baffled by wildlife organisations that seemed 'dedicated to a project that can only

➡

damage the Scottish countryside'. He points to evidence from as far afield as Patagonia,
35 New England, Norway and the upper reaches of the Danube which shows that beavers
pose a significant threat to woodland and river banks, destroying trees such as aspen and
oak, leading to the flooding of farmland and the disruption of salmon rivers.

What seems common to most conservation bodies is the way that they tend to discount
objections from people who live in the countryside. In similar fashion, the Royal Society for
40 the Protection of Birds defends the reintroduction of sea eagles despite the objections of
farmers who complain that these vast birds of prey have been seizing their lambs.

It seems perverse, at a time when rural economies are under such pressure, that
conservation projects, whose objectives seem frivolous, should be pursued – and with such
febrile logic. At a fierce meeting in Argyll to discuss the issue of sea eagles recently, an
45 RSPB man came out with a startling argument: rejecting the suggestion that they took live
lambs, he said that evidence from the nest sites showed they ate fulmars instead. Now,
fulmars are a graceful and elegant species of seabird, whose own existence is by no means
secure. Yet here was a conservation spokesman arguing that a native bird was little more
than a larder for a newly introduced killer species. That strikes me not just as frivolous,
50 but irresponsible as well.

In the second passage, Libby Purves, writing in *The Times* newspaper in 2008, discusses a plan to
reintroduce sea eagles to Suffolk in England.

Passage 2

A new sight puzzles winter ramblers in East Suffolk: above the snowy fields that sweep
down to the River Blyth, there stands a bold hand-lettered sign declaring 'Say no to sea
eagles here'. Baffling, at first: not much point in saying 'no' to that flying fortress of the
bird world, the white-tailed sea eagle. It wouldn't listen. It would just hang up there, 8ft
5 wingspan spread on a thermal, taking your breath away.

That, however, is not what the 'no' is about. It is a cry raised by farmers, landowners and
level-headed bird-lovers who are horrified at a plan hatched by the quango Natural England
and the RSPB, who want to spend more than £600,000 to introduce the birds to Suffolk.
They claim 'vast' popular support – though you could doubt the validity of a sample of 500
10 people asked some saccharine question about whether they fancy seeing one. Mark Avery,
of the RSPB, says with that familiar tone of scorn for his own species: 'Man is the reason
they are missing, and it is for us to put that right.'

Enthusiasts insist that it is a 'reintroduction', on the grounds that sea eagles once lived
here. Nobody has actually proved that Suffolk is their ancestral homeland – there are some
15 uncertain eighteenth-century bones – and the RSPB, indeed, was last quoted as saying
feebly that 'sea eagles must have been here in Roman times'. In Roman times, however,
Suffolk was a wild, boggy, scantily occupied place; and if a passing eagle threatened to
starve your family by nicking a piglet or cleaning out your fishpond, you were allowed to
chuck things at it and chase it off to fish the vast acres for which humans had no use.

20 Things have changed. Suffolk – still beautifully lonely in parts – supports as many people
as the whole of England did two thousand years ago. They farm land, raise stock, drive
vehicles, gather, and generally get on with their lives. And many of these are horrified at
this piece of meddling, scenting a PR exercise more concerned with quangoid prestige.

25 Some fear for livestock, especially lambs, and endangered birds such as terns. Others talk more wildly of the threat to dogs and cats. But even discounting that, there are snags. Sea eagles have the highest category of legal protection. Exclusion zones can be declared around any nest, so that in a radius of 100m or more nobody can do anything at all. Not drive a tractor and trailer, not maintain a fence, not hold a long-advertised event or festival. Basically, if a sea eagle moves in on you, it is like having a member of the royal family with
30 his protection and surveillance team buy the house next door. Suffolk is roomy, but not like the Hebrides, or the vast fjords and marshes of continental Europe in which the eagles have resettled. It's a daft idea.

They know that, really. They're just showing off. An internal email from Natural England hails a 'major opportunity for Natural England to lead a high-profile "flagship species"
35 project that will highlight the organisation at the forefront of a major biodiversity delivery initiative … There is a small risk of conflict with both socioeconomic and nature conservation interests, but these would be effectively managed by risk assessment and contingency planning … A thoroughly planned and well-executed public relations strategy will maximise the potential positive publicity for the organisation.'

40 See? It's a greater white-tailed gimmick. Expensive, vainglorious and typical of a growing trend in the 'conservation' industry. Many of the bodies that claim that title are not preserving at all: they are fiddling, initiating, interfering. That is not conservation: it is gardening, on a large scale. Put a woodland here – oops, no, make it a heath – tell you what, let's build a wetland and bring some classy creatures in by van. Punters will like that.

45 And that's fine. There are many artfully designed wilderness reserves that nourish the spirit and provide grand walks on signposted paths. Good luck to them. Many fine birds owe it all to the RSPB. But in a largely man-made rural environment, 'conservation' is a euphemism for landscape gardening. And the two should have different rules.

Questions

Passage 1 Questions

1. Analyse how the writer's use of language in lines 1–3 creates a negative impression of 'the world of nature conservation'.   3
2. Re-read lines 4–25.
   a) In your own words, identify two reasons given by SNH for the reintroduction of the beavers.   2
   b) Explain in your own words why the writer does not approve of the project.   4
   c) Analyse how the writer's use of language in lines 21–25 emphasises his disagreement.   4
3. Identify in your own words the key differences in point of view between SNH and local people given in lines 26–37.   4
4. Explain ways in which, according to the writer, the RSPB is behaving like 'most conservation bodies'. Use you own words in your answer.   2
5. a) Explain how the example of the RSPB man's 'fulmars' speech is used to develop the writer's argument.   2
   b) Analyse how the writer's use of language in lines 42–50 makes clear his contempt for conservation projects and the people behind them.   4

Passage 2 Question

6. Both writers express their views about the behaviour of nature conservation organisations. Identify key areas on which they agree. In your answer, you should refer in detail to both passages.

   You may answer this question in continuous prose or in a series of developed bullet points.   5

PAPER 4 – SOCIAL NETWORKING

The following two passages focus on social networking.

The first passage is taken from Hansard (the formal written record of proceedings in the UK Parliament) and is part of a speech made to the House of Lords by Baroness Greenfield, an eminent neuroscientist.

Passage 1

What precisely is the appeal of social networking sites? First, there is the simple issue of the constraints of modern life, where unsupervised playing outside or going for walks is now perceived as too dangerous. A child confined to the home every evening may find at the keyboard the kind of freedom of interaction and communication that earlier
5 generations took for granted in the three-dimensional world of the street. But even given a choice, screen life can still be more appealing. Building a Facebook profile is one way that individuals can identify themselves, making them feel important and accepted. I recently had a fascinating conversation with a young devotee who proudly claimed to have 900 friends. Clearly, this is a way of satisfying that basic human need to belong, to be part of a
10 group, as well as the ability to experience instant feedback and recognition – at least from someone, somewhere – 24 hours a day.

At the same time, this constant reassurance – that you are listened to, recognised and important – is coupled with a distancing from the stress of face-to-face, real-life conversation. Real-life conversations are, after all, far more perilous than those in the cyber
15 world. They occur in real time, with no opportunity to think up clever or witty responses, and they require a sensitivity to voice tone and body language. Moreover, according to the context and, indeed, the person with whom we are conversing, our own delivery will need to adapt. None of these skills are required when chatting on a social networking site.

Although it might seem an extreme analogy, I often wonder whether real conversation in
20 real time may eventually give way to these sanitised and easier screen dialogues, in much the same way as killing, skinning and butchering an animal to eat has been replaced by the convenience of packages of meat on the supermarket shelf. Perhaps future generations will recoil with similar horror at the messiness, unpredictability and immediate personal involvement of a three-dimensional, real-time interaction.

25 I think all of this poses something of a threat to young minds. First, I would suggest that attention span is at risk. If the young brain is exposed from the outset to a world of fast action and reaction, of instant new screen images flashing up with the press of a key, such rapid interchange might accustom the brain to operate over such timescales. It might be helpful to investigate whether the near total immersion of our culture in screen
30 technologies over the last decade might be in some way linked to the threefold increase over this same period in prescriptions for the drug prescribed for 'hyperactive' youngsters with ADHD.

Related to this change might be a second area of potential difference in the young
21st-century mind – a much more marked preference for the here-and-now, where the
immediacy of an experience trumps any regard for the consequences. After all, whenever
35 you play a computer game, you can always just play it again; everything you do is
reversible. The emphasis is on the thrill of the moment, the buzz of rescuing the princess
in the game. No care is given for the princess herself – because there is none. Perhaps we
should be paying attention to whether such activities may result in a more impulsive and
solipsistic attitude.

40 This brings us to a third possible change – in empathy. One teacher of 30 years' standing
wrote to me that she had witnessed a change over the time she had been teaching in the
ability of her pupils to understand others. She pointed out that previously, reading novels
had been a good way of learning about how others feel and think, as distinct from oneself.
Unlike the game to rescue the princess, where the goal is to feel rewarded, the aim of
45 reading a book is, after all, to find out more about the princess herself.

Finally, it seems strange that in a society that is so concerned about 'invasion of privacy',
we are at the same time enthusiastically embracing the possible erosion of our privacy
through social networking sites. When all your private thoughts and feelings can be
posted on the internet for all to see, maybe Facebook makes you think about yourself
50 differently. Are we perhaps losing a sense of where we ourselves finish and the outside
world begins? With fast-paced, instant screen reactions, perhaps the next generation will
define themselves by the responses of others; hence the baffling current preoccupation
with posting an almost moment-by-moment, flood-of-consciousness account of your
thoughts and activities, however banal. I believe it is called Twitter.

In the second passage, Moses Ma, writing in the journal *Psychology Today* in March 2009, discusses
the psychology of Twitter.

Passage 2

Twitter has officially become the next big thing in terms of internet social phenomena,
so I can't resist writing about it … just like everyone else. If you've never used or even
heard of Twitter, don't worry, you're not alone. As of now, less than 10 per cent of internet
users actually use Twitter, but it's growing like crazy: visitors to Twitter increased 1382
5 per cent year-over-year, from 475,000 unique visitors in February 2008 to 7 million in
February 2009, making it the fastest-growing social media site in the world.

Essentially, Twitter is an automated service for the sharing of short 140-character
communications. You can send tweets from your mobile phone as well as your computer.
Pretty much every major celebrity has a Twitter channel, from Britney Spears to John
10 Cleese, as the system has become the promotional channel of choice.

In many ways Twitter is the killer app for killing time, filling any moment with useless
drivel: *boy, I love lightly scrambled eggs, appletini or dirty martini? reply now & tell me what I
should order, stop & shop is out of weightwatchers brownies, but price chopper has 'em.* Riveting
stuff, indeed.

→

15 More interesting, however, is how the Twitter system acts to fill a deep psychological need in our society. The unfortunate reality is that we are a culture starved for real community. For hundreds of thousands of years, human beings resided in tribes of about 30 to 70 people. Our brains are wired to operate within the social context of community – programming crucial for human survival.

20 However, the tribal context of life was subverted during the Industrial Revolution when the extended family was torn apart in order to move labourers into the cities. But a deep evolutionary need for community continues to express itself, through the feelings of community generated by your workplace, your church, your sports team, and now … the twitterverse. This is why people feel so compelled to tweet, to facebook or even to check 25 their email incessantly. We crave connection.

It's sometimes fascinating to look at Twitter in the context of Abraham Maslow's concept of a hierarchy of needs, first presented in his 1943 paper 'A Theory of Human Motivation'.

Maslow's hierarchy of needs is most often displayed as a pyramid, with the lowest levels of the pyramid made up of the most basic needs, and more complex needs at the top of the 30 pyramid. Needs at the bottom of the pyramid are basic physical requirements including the need for food, water, sleep and warmth. Once these lower-level needs have been met, people can move on to higher levels of needs, which become increasingly psychological and social. Soon, the need for love, friendship and intimacy become important. Further up the pyramid, the need for personal esteem and feelings of accomplishment become 35 important. Finally, Maslow emphasised the importance of self-actualisation, which is a process of growing and developing as a person to achieve individual potential.

Twitter aims primarily at social needs, like those for belonging, love and affection. Relationships, such as friendships, romantic attachments and families, help fulfil this need for companionship and acceptance, as does involvement in social, community or 40 religious groups. Clearly, feeling connected to people via Twitter helps to fulfil some of this need to belong and feel cared about.

An even higher level of need, related to self-esteem and social recognition, is also brought into play by Twitter. At its best, Twitter allows normal people to feel like celebrities. At its worst, it is an exercise in unconditional narcissism – the idea that others might actually 45 care about the minutiae of our daily lives. I believe that this phenomenon of micro-celebrity is driven by existential anxiety. *I tweet, therefore I am*. I matter, I'm good enough, I'm smart enough and, goddammit, *people like me!*

Questions

Passage 1 Questions

1. Identify in your own words three reasons the writer gives in lines 1–11 for the attraction of social networking.   3
2. Analyse how the writer's word choice in lines 12–18 makes clear the difference between 'face-to-face' conversations and 'those in the cyber world'.   4
3. Evaluate how effective you find the analogy in lines 19–24 in developing the writer's ideas. Refer in your answer to the ideas contained in the analogy and to the language used by the writer to express it.   4
4. Re-read lines 25–39.
   a) Explain in your own words in what ways the writer believes social networking is 'a threat to young minds'.   4
   b) Analyse how the writer's use of language in lines 33–39 conveys her disapproval of video games. You should refer in your answer to such features as word choice, tone, sentence structure …   4
5. Explain in your own words why the writer makes references to a 'princess' in lines 40–45.   3
6. Analyse how the writer's use of language in lines 46–54 conveys her disapproval of social networking. In your answer you should refer to such features as tone, sentence structure, word choice …   3

Passage 2 Question

7. Both writers express their views about social networking. Identify key areas on which they agree. In your answer, you should refer in detail to both passages.

   You may answer this question in continuous prose or in a series of developed bullet points.   5

PAPER 5 – CHRISTMAS

The following two passages focus on the way we celebrate Christmas.

In the first passage Madeleine Bunting, in an article published in *The Guardian* newspaper a few days before Christmas, wonders how long the 'traditional' Christmas can survive.

Passage 1

By this point in the run-up to Christmas, most women have a manic look in their eyes. We're hardly capable of intelligible conversation, and those smiles over the mulled wine and mince pies verge on the frantic. If you could peer into our brains, you'd find our synapses working overtime, burning up a power station's worth of mental energy puzzling
5 out what to buy for whom and when.

The two toughest bits of Christmas are thinking what someone would like as a present – and actually finding it. The former is the almost exclusive preserve of women; this is when we're expected to demonstrate those feminine skills of empathy and thoughtfulness. Christmas, for women, is hard emotional labour (with much of the credit going to a
10 mysterious, elusive man).

The blame lies first of all with the Victorians. They pretty much invented Christmas – trees, Santa Claus, puddings, turkeys, decorations, cards, presents, family togetherness – ingeniously turning what had become a sober religious feast into a great festival requiring months of preparation. If women were to be kept at home, they had to have something to
15 do. It had got worse by the middle of the 20th century: the restless housewife not only had her pudding and cake to make, but was fiddling with twigs and silver spray to make table decorations.

But the crucial point about the Victorian Christmas, which always gets overlooked, is that it was only the middle classes who had one and it depended on a large amount of servant
20 labour. Now we have the near-impossible task of putting on the show single-handed. Add in a hundred or so years of consumer culture and its massive inflation of present expectations, and the formula is designed to produce an epidemic of seasonal migraines and divorces.

Yet the intriguing thing is how we all still struggle to deliver an essentially 19th-century
25 festival. We've never modernised Christmas; the only significant contribution the 20th century made was TV. It's a great tribute to the Victorians that we still have such a deep attachment to their creation.

It's lasted this long because many of the reasons that made the Victorians make such a big deal of Christmas are even more in evidence now. The Victorian rebranding was a response
30 to industrialisation: the family was no longer the wealth-producing unit; people were swapping working at home for factories and offices; urbanisation was disrupting the old

35 domestic structures. Social relations needed strengthening, so the home was relaunched with rituals such as regular family meals and the Sunday lunch. Home was idealised as a sanctuary from competitive market capitalism – a place where vulnerability, innocence and sentiment could be safely expressed. At the same time, childhood was idealised as a life-stage free of responsibility, a time of imagination, magic and enchantment. All of this came neatly together in the rituals the Victorians developed for Christmas.

40 The tougher the rigours of market capitalism have become, the more fuss we've made of Christmas. The more fragmented and dispersed families have become, the more the majority of us relish the annual dream of togetherness (and are bitterly disappointed when it doesn't match up). The harder we work, the more we want to create the perfect children's Christmas. The more our children's lives are institutionalised and regimented – in nurseries, in mugging up for tests – the more we want to give them an experience of magical enchantment. The more we worry about their safety, the more intensely we
45 want to celebrate innocence; after news of another sickening child abduction, we all need Christmas.

It's a form of emotional bulimia. Instead of a year punctuated by festivals, each with different traditions and all the cause for great eating, drinking and merry-making – as in Catholic Europe and most peasant cultures – Anglo-Saxon capitalism disciplined the
50 festive impulse into one brief period; presumably, it ensured factory routine was not disrupted year-round by drunkenness.

In the second passage, the novelist Terence Blacker, writing in *The Independent* newspaper, reflects on the effect Christmas has on the book trade … and on families.

Passage 2

The vast majority of new books published in the UK are sold at Christmas-time: bookshop sales in the last two months of last year were worth £264 million (nearly 30 per cent of the £960 million total for the year); turnover in December is almost five times what it is in April.

But as anyone who writes serious books for a living will know, the two months preceding
5 Christmas, the boom-time for bookshops, are also, by a strange paradox, a disastrous time in which to have a new book published, because the tender shoots of quality fiction, literary biography or sophisticated poetry are invariably crushed underfoot by a bellowing herd of the great TV-reared beasts of the publishing jungle – the glossy cookery books, the semi-literate sporting autobiographies, the TV gardeners and the celebrity explorers – as
10 they stampede towards the check-out tills.

There is something culturally depressing about this trend. It seems to confirm that, as an industry, publishing depends financially on the shifting of books as safe, acceptable objects for giving. A book looks good and feels nice, it tends to flatter the recipient in some way, but the vast majority of those given as presents will find their way on to the shelf or
15 coffee table or seat beside the loo after no more than a polite glance through their pages.

But perhaps here, unusually, the book business is revealing a wider sickness. One does not have to be a miserablist Scrooge to wonder whether the increasing hysteria that surrounds Christmas as a time for giving, for gathering together, for repairing fragile relationships that have been ignored throughout the year, is entirely healthy or sane. →

20 We are entering the period in the year when the words 'What are you doing for Christmas?' are to be heard throughout the land. They are rarely spoken with the joy of anticipation. Panicky family plans about how to deal with the problem aunt or the oddball cousin tend to have little to do with love and much to do with a rather dreary form of duty.

25 Maybe it is inevitable. We lead busy, selfish lives. An arrangement that shoe-horns the demands of extended family life into a few fraught, emotional, highly expensive days has brisk contemporary tidiness to it. Under this system, children who have been ignored can be showered with presents, marriages that are drying up can be irrigated with booze, relations who have been forgotten can be appeased with food and fake cheer. It may be tiresome but at least, come January, the duty is over for another year.

30 No wonder that for so many people, the fortnight at the end of the year is a time not of love or reassurance, but of stress and loneliness. Maybe it is time for us to wean ourselves off the excess of the Christmas habit, to try to spread the giving, the time spent with family, the parties, the general bonding of relationships throughout the rest of the year. As in the book trade, more is lost than is gained in placing all one's efforts and expenditure into one
35 brief, feverish moment during the year.

For the truth is that there is one significant economic sector whose business bonanza occurs not in November or December, but in January, after the decorations have come down. Wills are changed, petitions for divorce filed – the Christmas boom-time comes late for our learned friends the lawyers.

Questions

Passage 1 Questions

1. Re-read lines 1–10.
   a) Explain why, according to the writer, Christmas is particularly hard for women.   2
   b) By referring to more than one example, analyse how the writer creates a light-hearted tone in these lines.   2
2. Re-read lines 11–23.
   a) Identify in your own words the features of modern life that make it hard to replicate a Victorian Christmas today.   3
   b) Analyse how the writer's word choice and sentence structure make clear her view of the Victorians and the Christmas celebrations they created.   4
3. Re-read lines 24–46.
   a) Identify in your own words the key points of the writer's argument in lines 24–37 that the 'rituals the Victorians developed for Christmas' were 'a response to industrialisation'.   4
   b) Explain in your own words the reasons the writer gives in lines 38–46 for making a 'fuss' of Christmas.   4
   c) Analyse how the sentence structure of lines 38–46 emphasises the point that the writer is making in the paragraph.   3
4. Evaluate the effectiveness of the final paragraph (lines 47–51) as a conclusion to the passage as a whole. You should refer in your answer to ideas and to language.   3

Passage 2 Question

5. Both writers express their views about the way we celebrate Christmas. Identify key areas on which they agree. In your answer, you should refer in detail to both passages.

   You may answer this question in continuous prose or in a series of developed bullet points.   5

PAPER 6 – SHOPPING

The following two passages focus on shopping and consumerism.

In the first passage Neal Lawson, writing in *The Herald* newspaper, discusses our addiction to shopping.

Passage 1

We are caught up on a treadmill of turbo-consumption powered by the unfounded belief that having more will make us happy. We are part and parcel of a consumer society whose credentials are becoming more tarnished.

5 Increasingly, the predominant thing that you and I do is to shop and plan our lives around things we have to pay for: the clothes, jewellery, cars, houses, holidays, restaurants and gadgets that make us what we are. Once we were a society of producers, knowing ourselves and each other by what we did and what we made. Not any more. Today we understand ourselves and project the image we want others to see through what we buy.

Even for those who pretend they are above fashion, every item they own is based on finely
10 calibrated decisions about who and what they are and what they want others to think of them. With every purchasing decision, they reject thousands of other options, on other parts of the shelf, in other shops, in order to home in on the object that is 'them'. It might not be 'fashion' but it is *their* fashion. Today we are all what we drive and what we wear. We don't own things – they own us.

15 So what keeps us running on the consumer treadmill? We buy freedom, escape, love, care, excitement and comfort. We buy to belong to a particular social group and stand apart from others. And, of course, we buy status. We want to be as near the top of the herd as possible. Endless consumption fuels the instinct to be 'the best', to covet the newest car, to wear the latest outfit, to travel to ever-more exotic places, to possess the latest gadgets
20 and to own a prestigious home in a 'desirable' area.

The whole show is kept going by the vast laboratory of designers, producers, marketers, advertisers, branding experts, psychologists and retail consultants who devise the machinery for the image factory that defines the 21st century. The best brains in the world are engaged in continually engineering new wants into new needs: more and more things
25 we must have in order to be 'normal'.

But life on the treadmill is catching up with us.

Most frightening of all is the fact that there are so few other ways of expressing our humanity, so we increasingly take comfort in so-called 'retail therapy'. Yet the object of the sellers is to make us not satisfied but dissatisfied so that we soon go back for more.
30 Shopping rewards us just enough to leave space for more … and the emptier we feel the more we shop. It is the most vicious of vicious circles, and the paradox at the heart of Western society, which is based on the pursuit of 'more'.

→

35 How, then, do we escape from the treadmill of consumerism? There is no going back to some rose-tinted pre-consumption era. Shopping isn't all bad, after all – it's an important means by which we can be sociable and creative. However, we need to strike a balance, and that means regaining control over a marketing machine that has the sole purpose of making ever greater profits. We require a more compelling vision of what it means to be free and live a good life. Shopping sells us a powerful myth of liberty: that the car sets us free on the open road, for instance, when the reality is that we spend hours sitting in

40 choking traffic jams that get us nowhere and pollute the environment. We must grasp the fact that what we really need and cherish cannot be bought.

Perhaps the state needs to step in, and we must demand that it legislates to help us rebalance our lives as social beings and citizens, rather than simply as shoppers. A good start would be legal restrictions on advertising – particularly to children, who shouldn't

45 be subjected to the full force of the branding psychologists. Just as Sweden has banned advertising to under-12s, we need to do the same.

Other governmental measures could include increased taxation on luxury goods – thus signalling that status isn't gained by buying top-end merchandise. Finally, happiness – not wealth – must become the number one priority, which means replacing the GDP (gross

50 domestic product) with GWB (general wellbeing) as a measure of the nation's prosperity. The quality of our lives, not the quantity of our consumption, should be the measure of political success.

In the second passage, which is taken from the first chapter of a book on design, *The Language of Things* by Deyan Sudjic, a commentator on architecture and design, the writer discusses the importance of design in influencing purchasing decisions.

Passage 2

To start with the object that is closest to hand, the laptop on which I write these words was bought in an airport shop. There is no one but me to blame for my choice. Some shops are designed to seduce their customers. Others leave them to make up their own minds. Dior and Prada hire prize-winning architects to build stores on the scale of Grand Opera

5 to reduce shoppers to an ecstatic consumerist trance. Not airports. A generic discount electronics store at Heathrow is no place for the seductions, veiled or unveiled, of the more elaborate forms of retailing.

Yet even in an airport, buying is no simple, rational decision. Like an actor performing without makeup, stripped of the proscenium arch and footlights, the laptop that

10 eventually persuaded me that I had to have it did it all by itself. It was a purchase based on a set of seductions and manipulations that was taking place entirely in my head. And to understand how the laptop succeeded in making me want it enough to pay to take it away is to understand something about myself, and maybe a little about the part that design has to play in the modern world.

15　By the time I reached the counter, even if I didn't know it, I had already consigned my old Apple computer to the electronics street market in Lagos where redundant hard drives go for organ harvesting. Yet my dead laptop was no time-expired piece of transistorised Neolithic technology. In its prime it had presented itself as the most desirable and most knowing piece of technology that I could ever have wanted. It was a computer that had

20　been reduced to the aesthetic essentials. Just large enough to have a full-size keyboard, it had a distinctive, sparely elegant ratio of width to depth. The shell and the keys were all white.

Apple's designers were quick to understand the need to make starting a computer for the first time as simple as locating the 'on' switch. They have become equally skilled at

25　manipulating the exterior design to create visual obsolescence. They take the view that Apple's route to survival in the PC-dominated world is to use design as a lure to turn its products into aspirational alternatives to what its competitors are selling. It expects to sell fewer machines, but it charges more for them. This involves serial seduction. The company has to make the most of its customers so hungry for a new product that they will throw

30　away the last one every two years.

At Heathrow, there were two Apple models to choose from. The first was all white, like my last one. The other was the matt black option. Even though its slightly higher specification made it more expensive, I knew as soon as I saw it that I would end up buying it. The black version looked sleek, technocratic and composed. The purist white of my last one

35　had seemed equally alluring when I bought it, but the black one now seemed so quiet, so dignified and chaste by comparison. The keys were squares with tightly radiused corners, sunk into a tray delicately eroded from the rest of the machine. The effect was of a skilfully carved block of solid, strangely warm, black marble, rather than the lid on top of a box of electronic components.

40　Black has been used over the years by many other design-conscious manufacturers to suggest seriousness, but it was a new colour for Apple. Black is a non-colour, used for scientific instruments that rely on precision rather than fashion to appeal to customers. To have no colour implies that you are doing would-be customers the honour of taking them seriously enough not to try fobbing them off with tinsel. Of course this is precisely

45　the most effective kind of seduction.

And in the end black too becomes an empty signal, a sign devoid of substance, and I will no doubt fall for the next model that sets out to seduce me with its exclusive and tasteful credentials.

Questions

Passage 1 Questions

1. Re-read lines 1–14.
   a) Identify in your own words the key criticisms the writer makes of the way we live today.   4
   b) Analyse how the writer's word choice in lines 1–3 emphasises his low opinion of 'consumer society'.   2
   c) Analyse how the writer creates a critical tone in lines 9–14 about those who say they are 'above fashion'.   2
2. Re-read lines 15–20.
   a) According to the writer, what **two** key aspects of our lives do we attempt to satisfy by 'running on the consumer treadmill'?   2
   b) Analyse how the writer's sentence structure in these lines emphasises the points he is making.   4
3. Analyse how the writer's imagery in lines 21–25 conveys his view of how 'The whole show' is organised.   4
4. According to the writer in lines 37–41, what are the problems with our dependence on 'retail therapy' and what solutions does he suggest?   4
5. By referring to lines 42–52, identify in your own words the **three** measures the writer suggests the Government should take to 'help us rebalance our lives'.   3

Passage 2 Question

6. Both writers express their views about consumerism. Identify key areas on which they agree **and** on which they disagree. In your answer, you should refer in detail to both passages.

   You may answer this question in continuous prose or in a series of developed bullet points.   5

ACKNOWLEDGEMENTS

The Publishers would like to thank the following for permission to reproduce copyright material:

Photo credits page 5 © Martin M303/Fotolia; page 11 REX/Jane Hobson; page 17 © The Scotsman Publications Ltd/ Scran; page 25 © duncanandison/Fotolia; page 32 © ADRIAN DENNIS/AFP/Getty Images; page 42 © age fotostock / Alamy; page 63 © Hulton-Deutsch Collection/CORBIS; page 66 © travelib / Alamy; page 69 © Lintao Zhang/Getty Images; page 79 © NASA; page 83 © Zefrog / Alamy; page 84 © Moviestore collection Ltd / Alamy

Chapter opener image reproduced on pages v, 1, 2, 7, 13, 34, 39, 47, 62, 63, 66, 69, 72, 73, 81, 92, 102, 103, 107, 111, 114, 118, 121 © contrastwerkstatt – Fotolia.

Acknowledgements *Politics or technology – which will save the world* by David Runciman, published by Profile Books (pp3–4); 'How Harry Potter saved one small Highland town's economy' by Ian Jack in *The Guardian* 7 June 2014. Copyright Guardian News & Media Ltd 2014 (pp5–6); 'Beyond a joke' by Steven Poole in *The Guardian* 25 June 2014. Copyright Guardian News & Media Ltd 2014 (pp7–8); 'Sometimes it is right to wipe out a species' by Matt Ridley in *The Times* 26 May 2014 © The Times/News Syndication 2014 (pp9–10); 'Heard the one about women on TV?' by Victoria Coren-Mitchell in *The Observer* 27 July 2014. Copyright Guardian News & Media Ltd 2014 (pp11–12); 'Doctor, I feel slightly funny' by Phil Hammond in *The Independent* August 2002 © The Independent (pp14–15); The poem, 'Sounds of the Day' by Norman MacCaig is taken from *The Poems of Norman MacCaig*. Published by Polygon, an imprint of Birlinn Ltd (p17); *Summit Fever* by Andrew Greig, published by Canongate, 2005 (p18); *At the Loch of the Green Corrie*. Copyright © Andrew Greig 2010. Reproduced by permission of Quercus Editions Limited and Capel & Land Ltd (p19); 'The Telegram' by Iain Crichton Smith is taken from *The Red Door, The Complete English Stories 1949–1976*. Published by Birlinn Ltd (p21); 'Bilingualism is good for you. But monoglots needn't despair' by David Shariatmadari in *The Guardian* 6 June 14. Copyright Guardian News & Media Ltd 2014 (pp22–23); 'A seatbelt that stops me dozing off at the wheel? Baaa humbug to that' by David Mitchell in *The Observer* 27 July 14. Copyright Guardian News & Media Ltd 2014 (pp25–26); 'Toys traumatic toys' by Tom Shields in *The Herald* 13 June 2013 © Herald & Times Group (p28); Out of office reply: I'm on hols but please keep me up to speed' by Matt Rudd in *The Times* Aug 2014 © The Times/News Syndication 2014 (p30); 'Television criticism 16/08/2014' by A.A. Gill in *The Sunday Times* 16 August 2014 © The Sunday Times/News Syndication 2014 (pp32–33); 'Car trips are bad trips' by Stephen Bayley in *The Guardian* 07 June 2014. Copyright Guardian News & Media Ltd 2014 (pp34–35); 'Summer days and doing nothing' by Tim Lott in *The Guardian* 1 August 2014. Copyright Guardian News & Media Ltd 2014 (pp36–37); 'Invasive species' by Robert McKie in *The Observer* 24 August 2014. Copyright Guardian News & Media Ltd 2014 (p40); 'We wanted the web for free – but the price is deep surveillance' by John Naughton in *The Observer* 24 August 2014. Copyright Guardian News & Media Ltd 2014 (p40); 'Out of love with football? ' by Hugh MacIlvanney in *The Sunday Times* 23 October 2011 © The Sunday Times/News Syndication 2011 (p42); 'Proof at last: being fat is not our fault' by Sylvia Patterson in The Herald 10 April 2010 © Herald & Times Group (p43); 'BBC is shutting out young Britain' by Ian Bell in *The Sunday Herald* 9 March 14 © Herald & Times Group (p44); 'The madness of crowds' by A.C. Grayling originally appeared in *Prospect Magazine*, September 2014 © Prospect Magazine (p45); 'The New Age of Fracking, and how it Threatens Scotland's Dream of a Clean, Green Future' by Joyce McMillan in *The Scotsman* 15 February 2013 © The Scotsman Publications Ltd. (pp63–65); 'The year of living all too comfortably' by Katie Grant in *The Scotsman* 7 March 2005 © Katie Grant (pp66–68); Tony Parsons/GQ © The Condé Nast Publications Ltd. (pp69–70); 'TV matters: celebrity talent shows' by Mark Lawson in *The Guardian* 7 September 2011. Copyright Guardian News & Media Ltd 2011 (pp73–74); 'Strictly Come Dancing: who would join Pippa Middleton in your ideal lineup?' by Michael Hogan in *The Guardian* 28 June 2011. Copyright Guardian News & Media Ltd 2011 (pp73–74); 'Does man flu really exist?' by Barry Didcock and Ali Howard in *The Herald* 28 March 2010 © Herald & Times Group (pp75–76); 'Is the use of CCTV cameras in schools out of hand?' by Nick Pickles and Stephanie Benbow in *The Guardian* 12 September 2012. Copyright Guardian News & Media Ltd 2012 (pp77–78); 'Kennedy assassination: memory and myth refuse to die after 50 years' by Jonathan Freedland in *The Guardian* 22 November 13. Copyright Guardian News & Media Ltd 2013 (p79); 'Kennedy's Legacy of Inspiration' by Robert Dallek from *The New York Times*, 21 November 2013 © The New York Times. All rights reserved. Used by permission and protected by the Copyright Laws of the United States. The printing, copying, redistribution, or retransmission of this Content without express written permission is prohibited (p80); '1914: the Great War has become a nightly pornography of violence' by Simon Jenkins in *The Guardian* 4 August 2014. Copyright Guardian News & Media Ltd 2014 (pp81–82); 'Sombre TV moments' by Grace Dent in *The Independent* 5 August 2014 © The Independent (pp82–83); 'The Depressing Reality of Jury Service' by Matthew Lewin in *The Independent* 4 February 2004 © The Independent (pp84–86); 'Serving on a Jury Restored my Faith in Humanity' by Mark Steel in *The Independent* 12 February 2004 © The Independent (pp86–87); 'Sports days when losing is a winner' by Jackie Kemp in *The Herald* 4 June 2003 © Herald & Times Group (pp88–89); 'Training ground for no-goals mediocrity' by Gillian Bowditch in *The Scotsman* 6 April 2004 © The Scotsman Publications Ltd. (pp89–90); 'Put the Fear of God into these Thugs' in *The Telegraph* 8 May 2005 © Jenny McCartney/Telegraph Media Group Limited (pp93–94); 'In Praise of the Lowly Teenager' by Kate Figges in *The Times* 10 May 2004 © The Times/News Syndication 2004 (pp94–95); 'Once Upon a Time We Told Our Children Stories' by Michael Morpurgo in *The Times* 3 March 2005 © Michael Morpurgo (pp96–97); 'Thou Shalt Read' in *The Telegraph* 13 November 2005 © Anthony Horowitz/Telegraph Media Group Limited (pp97–98); 'Why should sex education just be duty of schools?' by Joyce McMillan in *The Scotsman*